Assimilation v. Integration in Music Education

Assimilation v. Integration in Music Education engages with an existential question for American conservatories and orchestras: What does it mean to diversify Western classical music? Many institutions have focused solely on diversifying the demography of their participants, but without a deeper conversation about structural oppression in classical music, this approach continues to isolate and exclude students of color. Rooted in the author's experience working with BIPOC (Black, Indigenous, and People of Color) students at a major American conservatory, this book articulates the issues facing minority students in conservatories and schools of music, going beyond recruitment to address the cultural issues that alienate students. The author argues that the issue of diversity should be approached through the lens of aesthetics, and that the performance and pedagogy of Western classical music must change if a more diverse membership is to thrive in this genre.

Reflecting on the author's experience through the lens of recent critical theory in music education, this volume presents the viewpoints of Black and Latinx music students in their own words. Addressing the impact of racialized aesthetics on the well-being of BIPOC music students, the author shows how students are alienated when attempting to assimilate into conservatory environments and envisions an alternative, integrative approach to conservatory education. Offering a deep dive into the psychological and cultural reasons for the racialization of Western classical music, and potential institutional solutions, this concise book is relevant to performers, students, and institutional leaders.

Christopher Jenkins is Associate Dean for Academic Support at the Oberlin Conservatory of Music, where he is Conservatory Liaison to the Office of Equity, Diversity, and Inclusion, and Deputy Title IX Coordinator. He holds master's degrees in viola performance and international affairs and public policy, and is completing a PhD in historical musicology from Case Western Reserve University, and a DMA in viola performance from the Cleveland Institute of Music.

CMS Emerging Fields in Music
Series Editor: Mark Rabideau, University of Colorado, Denver, USA
Managing Editor: Zoua Sylvia Yang, DePauw University, USA

The *CMS Series in Emerging Fields in Music* consists of concise monographs that help the profession re-imagine how we must prepare 21st Century Musicians. Shifting cultural landscapes, emerging technologies, and a changing profession in-and-out of the academy demand that we re-examine our relationships with audiences, leverage our art to strengthen the communities in which we live and work, equip our students to think and act as artist-entrepreneurs, explore the limitless (and sometimes limiting) role technology plays in the life of a musician, revisit our very assumptions about what artistic excellence means and how personal creativity must be repositioned at the center of this definition, and share best practices and our own stories of successes and failures when leading institutional change.

These short-form books can be either single-authored works, or contributed volumes comprised of 3 or 4 essays on related topics. The books should prove useful for emerging musicians inventing the future they hope to inhabit, faculty rethinking the courses they teach and how they teach them, and administrators guiding curricular innovation and rebranding institutional identity.

Inclusive Music Histories
Leading Change through Research and Pedagogy
Ayana O. Smith

Assimilation v. Integration in Music Education
Leading Change toward Greater Equity
Christopher Jenkins

For more information, please visit: www.routledge.com/CMS-Emerging-Fields-in-Music/book-series/CMSEMR

Assimilation v. Integration in Music Education
Leading Change toward Greater Equity

Christopher Jenkins

First published 2024
by Routledge
605 Third Avenue, New York, NY 10158

and by Routledge
4 Park Square, Milton Park, Abingdon, Oxon, OX14 4RN

Routledge is an imprint of the Taylor & Francis Group, an informa business

© 2024 Taylor & Francis

The right of Christopher Jenkins to be identified as author of this work has been asserted in accordance with sections 77 and 78 of the Copyright, Designs and Patents Act 1988.

All rights reserved. No part of this book may be reprinted or reproduced or utilised in any form or by any electronic, mechanical, or other means, now known or hereafter invented, including photocopying and recording, or in any information storage or retrieval system, without permission in writing from the publishers.

Trademark notice: Product or corporate names may be trademarks or registered trademarks, and are used only for identification and explanation without intent to infringe.

Library of Congress Cataloging-in-Publication Data
Names: Jenkins, Chris (Christopher) author.
Title: Assimilation v. integration in music education : leading change toward greater equity / Christopher Jenkins.
Description: New York : Routledge, 2024. | Series: CMS emerging fields. Leading change | Includes bibliographical references and index. |
Identifiers: LCCN 2023016172 (print) | LCCN 2023016173 (ebook) | ISBN 9781032107837 (hardback) | ISBN 9781032107868 (paperback) | ISBN 9781003217053 (ebook)
Subjects: LCSH: Music–Instruction and study–Social aspects. | Conservatories of music–Social aspects. | Assimilation (Sociology) | Music–Philosophy and aesthetics. | Social integration. | Music and race. | Culturally relevant pedagogy. | Discrimination in education. | Discrimination in the music trade.
Classification: LCC MT1.J38 A77 2024 (print) | LCC MT1.J38 (ebook) | DDC 780.71–dc23/eng/20230612
LC record available at https://lccn.loc.gov/2023016172
LC ebook record available at https://lccn.loc.gov/2023016173

ISBN: 978-1-032-10783-7 (hbk)
ISBN: 978-1-032-10786-8 (pbk)
ISBN: 978-1-003-21705-3 (ebk)

DOI: 10.4324/9781003217053

Typeset in Times New Roman
by Newgen Publishing UK

To my students.

Contents

List of Figures	*viii*
Series Foreword	*ix*
Acknowledgments	*xii*
Introduction	1
1 Assimilation in Conservatory Education	6
2 Transforming the White Racial Frame	27
3 Concrete Advice for Leadership and Staff	46
4 Equity	62
5 Interviews with Young Professionals	78
Conclusion	111
Index	*116*

Figures

1.1	Carlisle Indian School Band posed at the bandstand in 1901.	15
1.2	Carlisle Indian School Music Class, 1901.	16
1.3	Zitkála- Šá, circa 1898.	17
2.1	Philip Ewell.	29
2.2	Highly Reductive Sonata Form Cartoon.	31
2.3	Photo of a typical poster of white, male, European composers.	35
2.4	Portrait of William Grant Still, circa 1949.	40
4.1	Equity v. Equality.	63

Series Foreword

Emerging Fields in Music Series

Music is embraced throughout every culture without boundaries. Today, an increasingly connected world offers influence and inspiration for opening our imaginations, as technology provides unprecedented access to global audiences. Communities gather around music to mourn collective hardships and celebrate shared moments, and every parent understands that music enhances their child's chances to succeed in life. Yet it has never been more of a struggle for musicians to make a living at their art – at least when following traditional paths.

The College Music Society's *Emerging Fields in Music Series* champions the search for solutions to the most pressing challenges and most influential opportunities presented to the music profession during this time of uncertainty and promise. This series re-examines how we as music professionals can build relationships with audiences, leverage our art to strengthen the communities in which we live and work, equip our students to think and act as artist-entrepreneurs, explore the limitless (and sometimes limiting) role technology plays in the creation and dissemination of music, revisit our very assumptions about what artistic excellence means, and share best practices and our own stories of successes and failures when leading institutional change.

The world and the profession are changing. And so must we, if we are to carry forward our most beloved traditions of the past and create an audience for our best future.

Leading Change toward Greater Equity (a collection within the series) in a time of uncertainty and promise offers a comprehensive scaffolding of *why*, *what*, *how*, and *for whom* meaningful change is necessary if music schools are to equip students to invent the future they will soon inherit, offers faculty insights for rethinking the courses they teach and how they teach them, and recalibrates administrators' priorities, policies, and procedures as they paint the new landscape of the 21st century music school. The editor's premise for the collection is that institutions of higher learning in music must see their principal role as one that prepares musicians as one-of-a-kind artists-to-the-world, equipped with the requisite knowledge, skills, and understandings to create a lifetime of artistic moments, one after the next.

The collection begins by making the argument for music's "essential" place within the human experience as the foundation of professional and career development. It then offers and examines pillars for change by addressing three fundamental questions facing the profession:

Pillar 1: Whose music matters?
Pillar 2: What might be possible if we were to reposition creativity at the center of all that we do?
Pillar 3: How might individuals and communities, through the work of career musicians and the experience of music, become more joyful, hopeful, connected, and healthy through musical experience?

Each pillar opens with an anchor manuscript that provides a comprehensive approach for imagining change. Subsequent books within each pillar offer specific ways forward.

Finally, three books examine *how* the systems and eco-systems that drive our music schools maintain inequities and obstruct innovation. Examining the academic journeys of students, faculty, and administrators, the authors decode often invisible systems that limit our growth and offer opportunities to realign our words and actions with the goals of fighting for equity, fostering inclusivity, celebrating creativity, and embracing community and the joy inherent within music-making.

This book anchors Pillar 1: *Whose music matters?* and – by unpacking the historical racial assimilationist constructs within conservatories, offering strategies to deconstruct systemic white supremacy in classical music education so that we might create equitable infrastructures that support Black and Latinx students to thrive – sets the stage for discipline-specific change across music in higher education. Most powerfully of all, Christopher Jenkins humanizes his argument through the inclusion of recent music graduate testimonials that make clear the need for administrators, faculty, and students to lead change.

Acknowledgments

Deep thanks and appreciation go to Mark Rabideau, Genevieve Aoki, Susan McClary, Daniel Goldmark, and Philip Ewell; Andrea Kalyn, Mary K. Gray, and Bill Quillen; Lynne Ramsey and Jeff Irvine; Prudence and Lee Jenkins; and Anne, Anderson, and August.

Introduction

I moved to Ohio in the fall of 2014 to join Oberlin Conservatory as the Assistant Dean for Academic Support. The explicit purpose of this newly created position was to increase retention by enhancing academic support for all students. As a staff person of color, I found that many students of color would seek support from me. Soon, "Liaison to the Office of Equity and Diversity" was appended to my title, and I was trained as a Title IX Deputy Coordinator for the Conservatory. One of my jobs was to assist in the institutional process of determining whether a report of harassment and/or discrimination rose to the level of a policy violation. In this position, I spent several years hearing from conservatory students about their negative experiences. As a conservatory graduate, I already had a first-person view of the status and treatment of African-American conservatory students. Listening to students as they related their issues, day after day, provided me with an expansive perspective on the challenges faced by all conservatory students, but especially BIPOC and LGBTQ+ students in a conservatory environment.

Similar positions have since sprung up at music schools such as Juilliard, Yale, Eastman, and others, but this position was unusual at the time. Oberlin's early adoption of a new initiative in response to political and cultural upheaval aligns with its progressive history, although, like many predominantly white institutions, it is far from blameless in its historical treatment of students of color. Faculty and staff at small, progressive, predominantly white institutions are generally in the position of navigating fresh ideas and meeting student demands. At Oberlin, I found that student expectations were often just ahead of the curve. Young, progressive undergraduate students anywhere are often right for the wrong reasons, or wrong for the right reasons, but they are not completely wrong as often as some would like to believe.

In my first few months at Oberlin, students of color – and particularly those who self-identified as African-American and Latinx – would meet with me to describe social, musical, and academic experiences in which they felt excluded or alienated. These students came from a variety of backgrounds; some might have lived in entirely Black or Latinx environments before arriving at Oberlin, while others had spent at least some time in predominantly white musical training programs or racially mixed educational environments. Many of them felt it was necessary, to greater or lesser degrees, to suppress aspects of their cultural background that found no resonance in a conservatory environment. It was evident that providing access to conservatory education was not the same as providing adequate student support. The question was what "student support" should actually mean.

This book attempts to frame the experiences of many Black and Latinx students in conservatory environments as they related their own experiences to me, and to suggest changes that would improve the quality of those experiences. As an account of social, cultural, and musical observations from inside a Midwestern conservatory, this book is in the tradition of Bruno Nettl's *Heartland Excursions* and Henry Kingsbury's *Music, Talent, & Performance*, although it does not share their explicitly ethnomusicological approach. It also bears some similarity to oral history projects as the final chapter presents the narratives of Black and Latinx music students in their own words. I invite readers to begin this book by reading that chapter.

In my focus on domestic issues of race and class, this book shares some features with Anthony Abraham Jack's *The Privileged Poor* and Elizabeth Armstrong and Laura Hamilton's *Paying for the Party: How Colleges Maintain Inequality*, in which sociologists embedded themselves in universities for extended periods to observe the status of Black and/or low-income students. This book is distinct in that I was primarily an employee with a responsibility to students and the institution, rather than merely an observer. This vantage point likely renders my observations less objective, but provides additional insight because of my access to the inner mechanisms of policy and decision-making. I claim no specific research methodology, but intend to reframe the issue of student "support" filtered through personal experience, while offering practical advice for conservatories attempting to provide that support and advice for administrators interested in creating similar positions.

In his efforts to oppose the ideology of "absolute music" and culturally situate conservatory training, Kingsbury quotes ethnomusicologist John Blacking: "we must recognize that no musical style has 'its own terms': its terms are the terms of its society and culture."[1] Kingsbury published this in 1988, but conservatory culture, by and large, still takes for granted the universalist character of classical music. Universalist claims about the appeal and transmissibility of Western classical music values may not be 100% inaccurate in the long run; through experience, regardless of background, anyone in the world may indeed learn to understand and appreciate the artistry of a piano sonata by Ludwig van Beethoven.[2]

However, students of color – even those who are highly motivated to seek out a conservatory education – often find that some of classical music's values do not resonate with their lived experience. I suggest that this feeling is influenced by aesthetic friction – that the expectations of beauty in concert dress, formal speaking in class and on stage, and even in the production of musical sound draw primarily from aesthetic priorities of the dominant white culture.

The demographic makeup (called "demographic diversity") of matriculated students and new faculty members, and the identities of the composers whose music we choose to play, have been the main subjects in recent discussions about diversity in classical music. This view of diversity ignores the psychological and social assumptions about aesthetic ideals in musical, social, and academic behavior. These unarticulated aesthetics extend to conventions of speech, dress, hairstyle, the carrying of one's body, and written and verbal communication.

The thesis of this book is that while access programs and increased scholarships may change student demographics, aesthetic alienation is a fundamental issue because *the aesthetics of the conservatory environment do not resonate with many students of color. Educational programs that diversify student demographics without effecting their own pedagogical and aesthetic changes are programs of assimilation.*

While this may seem like a bold claim, there is a long history of assimilationist projects in American education. Some of these were oriented toward the arts; some were explicitly violent; and sometimes art and violence overlapped. These programs have required and continue to require students of color, to various degrees, to assimilate. This claim need not be essentialist either, as it does not suppose that every student of a specific racial background exhibits the same specific preferences.

It is important to frame race as a social invention and political tool. Race is imaginary, but culture is real; and yet, culture is intersectional and personal. Race cannot be determinant of anything because it is not real; and still, it is not wholly divorced from preferences and taste. Culture may align with racial categories as they are framed in any given society. Music programs that recruit students from a more diverse range of racial and cultural backgrounds have the best chance of improving retention and student success if they change internally. The arrival of a more diverse student body provides an opportunity to reconsider and reimagine the conservatory environment, making it more flexible, responsive, and diverse itself.

In philosophy, the term "aesthetics" refers to a concept of perfection or beauty. In the arts, it refers to an agreed-upon ideal. Conservatory education is all about the student's search for the ideal in developing technical and musical skill, to find the apex of performance. Musicians are entirely aware of the standards for an ideal musical interpretation and performance and for an ideal piece of writing or an ideal spoken presentation. But the concept of the ideal in performance extends to ideals within other domains of behavior, such as dress and speech, and then expands to include a wider range of *expected* or *preferred* behavior, rather than that only that which is ideal or the best.

The first chapter of this book presents the author's perspective on the aesthetic alienation experienced by students of color in conservatory environments. The second chapter examines social theories, such as the white racial frame, fugitive pedagogy, and assimilationist education, in the context of classical music. This chapter also problematizes the discussion of solutions. I warn against the dangers of "solutionism," in which institutional leaders, grappling with their own culpability in the perpetuation of structural racism, embrace short-term solutions. Solutionism allows institutions to check the "diversity" box for boards eager to say they have solved the problem of racism at their institutions. In the third chapter, I address the advantages and disadvantages, for institutions and for students, of creating a DEI center and/or a staff position intended to address issues of equity and belonging. I make suggestions for how such a position should be structured and for staff hired into those positions. The fourth chapter addresses questions of equity, which are often overlooked in conservatory education.

The fifth chapter presents edited transcripts of interviews with Black and Latinx graduates from conservatories or schools of music. The accounting of their experiences adds a personal element to the illustration of the challenges these students face in conservatory education.

Notes

1 Henry Kingsbury, *Music, Talent, and Performance: A Conservatory Cultural System* (Philadelphia, PA: Temple University Press, 1988), 16–17.
2 One issue with this universalist formulation is that some of its supporters suppose that not only can anyone in the world learn to appreciate Ludwig van Beethoven, but that those who seek social status in the Western world must do so because it is an indication of "intelligence" and "taste." In this way, the universalist formulation mimics a supremacist formulation.

1 Assimilation in Conservatory Education

Introduction

In the past few decades, organizations promoting Western classical music have begun to make more serious attempts to "diversify." I put this term in quotes because a satisfactory answer has not yet been proposed to what could be labeled the "diversity question": What does it really mean to diversify Western classical music?

One might wonder why it took so long for this question to be prioritized, since the right answer could be critical to Western classical music's survival. While the U.S. is projected to become a majority-minority nation by 2045, Western classical music audiences and performers remain mostly white. And, while much of Western classical music's diversification has been driven by increases in musicians and staff of Asian and Pacific Islander background, the percentage of the U.S. population identifying as Latinx or African-American continues to increase steadily. From the year 2000 to the year 2020, the number of U.S. counties in which people identifying as Hispanic accounted for the majority of the population doubled.[1] It is estimated that those who self-identify as being of Hispanic heritage will make up 29% of America's population by 2050.[2] (An increase in "racially mixed" couples is also responsible for an increase in the number of individuals claiming African-American heritage; between 2010 and 2020, the number of Americans identifying as "Black" and one other race increased by 230%.[3])

To diversify classical music, institutions have, focused on increasing the percentage of African-American and Latinx

DOI: 10.4324/9781003217053-2

participants. In 2021, orchestras with fellowships for African Americans included the Virginia Symphony, Cincinnati Symphony, and Detroit Symphony, among others. Programs focused on increasing the number of Black and brown music students and professionals presuppose that the answer to the question of diversification is primarily demographic: that diversity in Western classical music is defined by the demographic diversity of audiences, professional performers, composers, and students; that the color of participants' skin is the most important measure of classical music's diversity.[4]

There are many such access programs in an array of fields, ranging from STEM to chess, and even sports such as tennis and golf.[5] Racially targeted classical music access programs have great value because when successful, they increase access to training and significant musical experiences for marginalized groups and create professional entry points into a historically racist field. The growth of such programs should undoubtedly continue because they provide resources to historically marginalized populations and are likely to assist in countering racist attitudes among whites in classical music. At the same time, access to these environments is not the same thing as support. It is not a settled question as to what adequate support looks like.

Comprehensively addressing the issue of support requires us to raise significant questions about assimilation, cultural erasure, and decolonization, and the nature of the environments into which African-American and Latinx students are being invited. To articulate some of these questions: What if diversity is determined by content as much as demographics – not just of the music being performed, but the character of physical and social environments and the unspoken social rules governing the behavior of participants? What if content is defined not only by its creators' racial identity, but also through its embeddedness in cultural memory and communication of aesthetic values? What if how Western classical music is performed is at least as important as who performs it?

This book focuses on the experiences of African-American and Latinx students engaged in musical performance training at the college and graduate level. Its conclusions are based on my experiences as a conservatory associate dean working with this student population. Although these conclusions do not and cannot reflect the experiences of every music student in this group, the remarkable consistency, over time, of the issues reported by these students has convinced me that the accepted demographic approach to diversifying Western classical music is insufficient.

The argument advanced here is that the cultural norms, expectations, and ideals of American conservatories and schools of music reflect a design by and for a white majority. This design creates environments aligned with core values of Western classical music that are historically backward-facing and Eurocentric in nature. It is not too much to say that implicitly, these environments culturally reflect the values of white supremacy, not in the narrowly historical, limited sense of violent white nationalist groups, but in the broader sense of the assumption that the cultural values, historical figures, musical compositions, and social norms common to white Americans and Europeans are superior to others. The recruitment of students from different cultural backgrounds requires assimilation into an aesthetic environment that supposes a particular type of aesthetics to be superior and discounts the music and musical aesthetics of people of color.

Many others have observed that classical music elevates whiteness and encourages cultural erasure and assimilation. In 1995, Bruno Nettl wrote that, "There are some ways in which the music school functions almost as an institution for the suppression of certain musics."[6] In an open letter to music school leadership, Dylan Robinson has exhorted school leadership to yield control over to students of color, so that "rather than shaping IBPOC [Indigenous, Black, Latinx, Asian, and other people of color] to fit the program's goals, allow them to reshape the program and the forms of community in place."[7] Zach Ferriday notes that a classical music forum on the white supremacist website *Stormfront* features the comment "Listening to the classics FORCES you to be white."[8] If racial categories are truly real and fixed (as the average *Stormfront* reader would presumably believe) then people who are not white cannot, by definition, be forced to become so. Yet apparently, some ineffable quality of Western classical music "compels" whiteness. This commenter is cueing into something essential about the relationship between the social construction of whiteness and Western classical music's aesthetics.[9]

I also propose that theories of culturally responsive pedagogy, the white racial frame, and fugitive pedagogy in Black education are helpful tools in the identification and dismantling of oppressive structures embedded in classical music's performance and pedagogy. I draw upon my own personal experiences as a Black classical musician and as a conservatory staff member working with this student group to highlight potential negative outcomes for African-American and Latinx conservatory students in terms of their self-esteem, mental health, and racial attitudes. Naming and describing these oppressive structures is challenging but necessary. The concept of "habitus," developed by the French philosopher Pierre Bourdieu to refer to the social superstructures lying just on the edge of conscious perception, or "structuring structures," is a helpful frame.[10]

I suggest there is value in focusing on cultural aesthetics, the concept of the beautiful, because musicians are already self-selected as a group to prioritize aesthetic refinement as a professional goal. Students spend most of their time in conservatories in pursuit of the most beautiful sonic presentation they can elicit. But aesthetics also extend to dress, speech, stage presentation, and social interactions. It is the friction caused by differing conceptions of the "ideal" in both performance and daily life that I observe as a major cause of difficulty for many students of color.

The central implication of conservatory pedagogy, curriculum, performance styles, repertoire, and social environments – that white aesthetic preferences are superior – devalues the identities and personhood of students of color. To assimilate into a structure that assumes the inferiority of yourself and people like you requires a violent self-negation that many students of color bear unconsciously and never acknowledge.

> *Classical music is such a weird environment. You go to a concert, you can't clap at these times, you can't be too loud, if you're cheering then you're the only one that's loud, and that's like, oh, no. It's just a strange thing. So, it can often be hard to get somebody to come to this hour-and-a-half long orchestra concert.*
> (African-American conservatory graduate)

Black and Latinx music students are hardly a monolithic group culturally or economically, and our experiences and backgrounds can be measured across a wide spectrum. Class identity plays a role in determining comfortability in classical music environments. In "'McDonald's Music Versus 'Serious Music,'" Anna Bull and Christina Scharff found that class was a major determinant of comfort with music defined as "classical" v. "urban," as well as with the spaces, dress, and modes of listening that dominate classical music.[11] Nettl observed that classical ensembles are designed to validate the very concepts of class difference and hierarchy, as orchestral seating mimics the organizational structures of the industrial factory, the military, and the plantation system, and chair assignments are taken as fixed assignations of personal and professional value.[12]

One of the musicians interviewed for this book mentioned that some minority students come to conservatories from solidly middle- or upper-class households in which they have already experienced a higher degree of interaction with, and perhaps assimilation into, mainstream white value systems. Other students may have been economically under-resourced, but have acculturated through access programs, allowing them to attend a private arts high school, or they have been provided other forms of expensive training putting them in touch with majority-white student populations. While acknowledging the potential economic and educational benefit for economically disadvantaged students of color who are given access to private Western classical music education, I would like to problematize the supposition that Western classical music education should be judged as an unambiguous benefit for students of color. I am suggesting a more balanced, and critical, view of racially-based access programs.

In *The Privileged Poor*, Anthony Abraham Jack distinguishes between students he characterizes as the "privileged poor," those from low-income backgrounds with experiences in largely white educational spaces through high school access programs, and the "doubly disadvantaged," low-income students admitted into privileged college environments but lacking previous intercultural experience or financial resources to help them adapt.[13] The privileged poor and students from middle-class or upper-class backgrounds have had access to high level music training and the cultural capital of concert attendance. They have experienced basic conversational and written modes of Western classical music criticism. The challenges faced by "doubly-disadvantaged" students and the "privileged poor" are often compounded by imposter syndrome and a fear that "inclusion" means that they have been accepted because they are of color and not because of their talent. A student with whom I work composed a poem that aptly communicates these feelings:

> *I played alone, never thinking beyond my broken home. Liquor St. and Colfax ave, reading down concrete escapades burned by bike pedals and bloodied afternoons. My paperback in hand of an intellectual freedom land; Lights, Camera, Violence down the stage to pews built in cultural silence– Capeless gowns and academic blues, was it my blackness that only mattered to you?*

It would be essentialist and inaccurate to say that all Black and Latinx students find conservatory and orchestral environments totally alienating. But it would also be inaccurate to say that most Black and Latinx students encounter conservatory environments totally free from prejudice, implicit bias, or microaggressions. The argument advanced here is more subtle but far-reaching: that the musical, social, and psychological values and norms enforced in a conservatory environment do not fully resonate with the cultural backgrounds of many African-American and Latinx students. Often, these students are only subconsciously aware of the nature of the issue they are experiencing because it has never been described for them, and as young people they may lack the experience or vocabulary necessary to fully articulate their personal experiences.

The bottom line is that it is relatively easy to be inculcated into a supremacist culture, even if that culture denigrates one's own background. In the absence of measures to change the aesthetic culture of Western classical music, inclusion starts to feel uncomfortably close to assimilation and erasure, both of which have historically been prominent features of American education.

Why African-American and Latinx Students? And Countering Essentialism

At Oberlin, I work with all students. But much of my work has involved low-income students, first-generation students, students with disabilities, and students who struggled socially, psychologically, and/or academically. Many of these students were African-American and/or Latinx. This book focuses on these students. It is important to acknowledge the limitations of this focus. It omits important portions of the BIPOC coalition. Discussions of bias in music education should acknowledge the historical and current discrimination faced by people of Asian descent in Western classical music. I recall a visit by an internationally renowned classical musician to my undergraduate school, where in front of a large audience he confidently announced his belief that people of Asian descent liked Western classical music because they were emotionally repressed, and its expressive nature negated the stultifying effect of their rigid "home" cultures. (He was met with a chorus of boos.) People of Asian descent face racism and microaggressions in conservatory environments, in orchestras, and in the larger world. Members of many other groups, including white students who may suffer from any number of disadvantages, will benefit from more robust support if they are to succeed in conservatories. (I address the issue of equity for all in chapter 4.)

It is important for conservatories to serve all students who are marginalized, but in this book, I choose to focus on African-American and Latinx students for several reasons. First, my personal and professional experiences have best positioned me to speak to the experiences of these students. Second, conservatories and orchestras are increasingly recruiting students and performers who identify as being in these categories.

Additionally, African-American identity has long been used as shorthand for "people of color." The entire concept of racial capitalism undergirding American's political economy arose out of white mistreatment of African Americans and Native Americans. As sociologist Joe Feagin notes, African-Americans have served as a central point of reference and cultural opposition for whites, the standard against which white culture defines itself. Until the 1950s, it was legal for whites to sue for defamation if they had been labeled as Black.[14]

But race is an invention, if an extraordinarily powerful one. It is a category that is political rather than biological, as evidenced by the distinctions between legal systems of racial categorization in different countries. Supposed racial differences have no basis in biology or behavior, and 99.9% of human genes are identical across racial categories.[15] Racial categories are useful political inventions because they rationalize unequal distributions of power and resources, both in terms of the measurable financial benefit and the "public and psychological wage" that accrue to whiteness.[16]

Culture, however, is real, unlike race, and cultural differences are not wholly imaginary. But culture is not affixed to imaginary racial categories; it is flexible and dynamic. No two people share perfectly identical cultural backgrounds. Those who identify as being of a certain race are not limited to the enjoyment of a particular musical aesthetic, nor will they inevitably play or hear music in a certain way. Race is an invention while culture is real; but culture is personal and intersectional. The essentialist needle can be threaded by rejecting the notion that the only essential differences between people align with racial categories, while still making space for the appreciation of cultural differentiation between groups; and acknowledging that the personal nature of culture allows for enormous differentiation within groups.

My two propositions are that conservatory education has assimilationist characteristics, and that it is useful to view its assimilationist character through the lens of aesthetics. These propositions are demonstrated through the historically assimilationist character of American education programs, and the role of music in these programs.

A lot of times, I didn't know all of the music jargon, the vocabulary needed to speak up in the classes. Maybe I know the answer, but I just don't have the words I don't have, so I didn't feel like it was worth talking a lot of the time. It wasn't until maybe my third year that I was, like, honestly, at this point, I couldn't care less what y'all think about me. By the time it felt like an act of revolution, just to speak the way that I would speak normally. I would come in and be like, that piece is boss, I mean, what you want me to say, it slaps and that's how it goes. And they're like, oh, okay.
(African-American conservatory graduate)

A Very Brief History of Assimilationist Education

There is a longstanding critique of American education as a assimilationist project. In his 1933 book *The Miseducation of the Negro*, Carter G. Woodson, the creator of Black History Month, proposed that the educational system for African Americans arising out of Reconstruction offered inadequate instruction because its principal aim was cultural indoctrination, rather than career preparation.[17] The use of Western classical music as an educational tool to promote cultural assimilation is not a new phenomenon. It was an essential component of one of the most explicit and violent assimilation programs, that of Native Americans at American and Canadian "Indian" schools, where curricula were explicitly designed to erase Native American cultural practices.

The first such school in the U.S., the Carlisle Indian Industrial School, was founded in Carlisle, PA in 1879. Its students are pictured in Figures 1.1 and 1.2. It imposed restrictions intended to culturally annihilate Native traditions, such as forced cutting of hair, required use of anglicized names, the forbidding of Native languages, and the forbidding of Native music in favor of instruction in Western art music from the baroque, classical, and romantic eras. Choirs of Native American students rehearsed Western classical pieces and performed them for various school functions and ceremonies. Abigail Winston, a researcher on the school, notes that school leaders cited Western music instruction as an important tool to facilitate assimilation by destroying Native musical traditions.[18]

The most musically accomplished Native American students who emerged from these schools were held up as exemplars of achievement and proof of the "civilizing" effect of Western music education. Zitkála-Šá, pictured in Figure 1.3, was a native woman who began violin lessons as a student at the Indiana Manual Labor Institute of Wabash, Indiana, and studied violin at the New England Conservatory (NEC) in the late 1890s. (NEC and Oberlin Conservatory were two of the few music schools accepting students of color at this time.) She later taught Western classical music at the Carlisle Indian School. In 1900, she was invited to perform for President William McKinley. Ultimately, she became a strong advocate for Native rights and a critic of the "Indian" schools, and founded the National Council of American Indians, one of the most important advocacy groups for Native people.[19] Profiles celebrating her musical talent should also grapple with the fact that her musical abilities were the result of a violent project of assimilation seeking to annihilate her cultural heritage.

According to Ibram X. Kendi, the historical impetus for inclusion of African Americans in white educational systems

Figure 1.1 Carlisle Indian School Band posed at the bandstand in 1901.
Source: Johnson (Frances Benjamin) Collection, Library of Congress.

was based on an assumption of inferiority rather than equality. White assimilationists and segregationists agreed about Black capability; both groups assumed that people with darker skin were uncivilized, incapable, and ignorant. But white assimilationists, considering themselves well-meaning, believed that people of color could be made better through inclusion in white educational systems. Kendi refers to this tendency as "uplift suasion," meaning that the success of the right kind of African Americans in white schools would convince whites that talented people of color could be "uplifted" through access to white environments. This belief extended to the point where white assimilationists thought that Blacks who were civilized in this way would actually change color and turn physically white. They pointed to the physical condition of vitiligo as evidence of this process.[20]

While this belief has faded, conservatories do expect students of color to modulate their speech, bodies, and behavior, and this burden falls unequally on students depending on prior cultural

Figure 1.2 Carlisle Indian School Music Class, 1901.

Source: Johnson (Frances Benjamin) Collection, Library of Congress.

familiarity. Students must be comfortable wearing tuxedos or other specific types of formal dress, carrying their bodies in a certain way on stage, interacting with audience members through a specific protocol, and generally speaking English with a particular style of diction, especially if they are singers. The term "inclusion" should be more closely questioned, given its historical definition in the context of assimilationist education programs as "providing access to inferior groups so as to facilitate their betterment."

On Aesthetics

I propose that aesthetics, a philosophy of the beautiful, is a useful framework to examine the racialization of music education. This is because the racialization of aesthetics is rarely acknowledged, and because serious music students have already self-selected as an aesthetically oriented group. Much has been published on the

Figure 1.3 Zitkála-Šá, circa 1898.

Source: National Portrait Gallery, Smithsonian Institution.

racialized and gendered nature of aesthetics, such as Paul Taylor's *Black Is Beautiful*. In *The Race of Sound*, Nina Eidsheim describes the biased expectations we make of vocal performers based on their race. Eidsheim's injunction is that "voice is not innate, it is cultural; voice is not unique, it is collective; voice's source is not the singer; it's the listener."[21] In "Deconstructing the Ideology of White Aesthetics," JM Kang writes

> Because Whites are the dominant group in America, they dictate what is beautiful. The consequence of this power dynamic is that the dominant group, Whites, can exercise preferences in deciding how to look or express themselves, whereas people of color are limited to either conforming to an imposed White standard or rejecting it.[22]

Kang is saying that as long as whites retain the autonomy to reshape norms and standards according to their own preferences, aesthetic assimilation is a condition of acceptance for people of color into majority-white spaces. Aesthetic autonomy is hazardous because it invites social and economic marginalization.

An example of this dynamic is evident in American clothing styles. For decades, mainstream tastemakers denigrated clothing styles categorized as "hip-hop influenced" or "street wear" that were popular among African-American youth. These styles only became desirable for the mainstream when white influencers began to imitate and appropriate them. Minh-Ha Pham of the Pratt Institute labels this phenomenon "racial plagiarism" as a replacement term for "cultural appropriation."[23] Because tastemakers and gatekeepers of the dominant group set standards that subordinate or exclude other aesthetics, members of other groups can either retain their aesthetic standards and risk exclusion, or assimilate. To varying degrees, many choose to alternate between the two. They express the aesthetic reflective of their home culture in their personal life, and adhere to the dominant aesthetic in the professional sphere and in mainstream social situations.

Kang notes that the psychic impact of this aesthetic subordination should not be discounted as trivial:

> Throughout America's history, the terms "beauty" and "truth" were either explicitly or implicitly employed in political rhetoric and judicial opinions in order to construct subordinating images of people of color, justify legal oppression, and perhaps most profoundly, produce an epistemology of racial bodily aesthetics that, to some degree, possibly alienated people of color from their own bodies because they failed to resemble those of White people.[24]

The term "beauty" is particularly relevant in the context of classical music. "Beauty" in sound production is one of the foremost concerns of classical music instruction. Characteristics of "beautiful" Western classical music sound are specific: sound must be rounded, vibrant, not harsh or aggressive, and attendant to the creation of a "smooth," "elegant," and "lyrical" musical line.

But the aesthetics of classical music extend beyond the sonic presentation. "Beauty" in self-presentation and stage presence is also prescribed. Hair, dress, and speech on stage conform to similar standards: hair will ideally be "smooth," clothes "elegant," speech and diction "precise." Clothing should retain maximum sex appeal within a moderately conservative standard (as evidenced by the outfits orchestral soloists often wear). Perhaps most challenging, and potentially degrading, the aesthetics of the body are also expected to conform to white standards, adhering to particular ideas about "elegance" and shape. Of course, while one's clothes, and diction can be altered to suit the tastes of another, similar manipulation of the body is far more challenging.

And unfortunately, this was the only part of my career, only part of my life, where I've really experienced just outward, clumsy racism, professionally...Especially for Black musicians, who are carrying a distinct, and I think, very valuable culture into these institutions – the institutions are not prepared to handle them. If there's no work rule that says you can't wear a dashiki and dreads at work, you should be able to do that. And unfortunately, we often find out that a person in power will object to it. And then that becomes the new rule, but it's not contractually obligated or written down anywhere, and still because you're the subordinate you need to abide by this rule.

(African-American orchestral musician)

A counter-argument to the foregrounding of aesthetics might be that because aesthetics are socially enforced through relative and unequal distributions of power, we're really talking about politics, and aesthetics are simply one of many political tools. It can be hard to sign on to the idea that something as artistically fluffy as *aesthetics* could so deeply affect our social worlds and hierarchies. Robin James proposes that aesthetics are central to the dissemination of power, writing that systems of privilege and oppression are the central vehicle through which society is organized, and that "White supremacy, patriarchy, or heteronormativity are political because they are aesthetic."[25]

Aesthetics are indeed a political tool, but not just any old tool. The toolbox of standard political manipulation includes relationships with and control over the media, donors, and redistricting. Aesthetics are a far more effective tool in enforcing oppressive systems because they operate in the background in determining social boundaries and expectations but are nearly impossible to identify.

Saying that aesthetics are racialized is not the same as signing on to racial determinism. But there is a measure of alignment between musical aesthetics, culture, and race. As the dance scholar Brenda Dixon Gottschild notes, "Since the first Africans and Europeans set foot on these alien, new world shores, their aesthetic preferences have offered a study in contrasts."[26] Gottschild observes five qualities unique to African-American swing music:

1. "Embracing the conflict," meaning to aim for a "noisy" sound quality, contrasting with the "clean" sound idealized in classical music.
2. "High-affect juxtaposition," presenting unrelated or even opposing moods or attitudes immediately and without transition, unlike the formalized transition from primary to secondary theme in classical sonata form.
3. "Ephebism," infusing every note with "quintessential vitality."
4. Prioritizing rhythm over melody and juxtaposing counterrhythms; the centrality of groove as opposed to the flexibility of tempo observed in classical music (speaking to a hierarchy of control; a groove is generated communally while tempo in classical music is often dictated by a single figure, in the person of the conductor or first chair).
5. "The Aesthetic of the Cool," performing with intensity and virtuosic flair while exuding a calm, even careless attitude.[27]

Olly Wilson, electronic music composer and founder of Oberlin's TIMARA department, describes six traditional characteristics of African-American music:

1. Use of rhythmical ambiguity and polyrhythm.
2. Instruments played for percussive effect and to create stress accents.
3. Call-and-response structures on multiple levels.
4. High musical-event density.

5 A "heterogeneous sound tendency" consisting of many voices of opposing timbres simultaneously.
6 The use of the physical body in making music.[28]

While there is considerable overlap between Wilson and Gottschild, two aesthetic qualities are particularly salient: the centrality of rhythm and the use of complex polyrhythm, and a focus on percussive sound quality.[29] These characteristics are in contradistinction with the aesthetics of Western classical music, particularly concerning rhythm and sound quality. Western classical training values a "clean" sound. High-musical event density, simultaneous heterogeneous sound timbres, and instruments played percussively create the opposite effect.

No one should believe that Black students have some genetic and innate understanding of these aesthetics (of course they do not) or that they are naturally compelled to make music in a certain way (of course they are not). However, these aesthetics inform the larger universe of Black music-making and Black sound with which Black students are likely to have greater familiarity. Some Black students may have been immersed in musical environments that foregrounded these aesthetics, while others may have had a passing experience with these styles of music in the background at home or with friends. But these aesthetics are likely to have been part of their sonic universe, and at some point they are likely to have observed that people like them tend to make a certain kind of music in a certain type of way, creating a linkage between perceived identity and sound production. The conservatory's implicit message that the aesthetic preferences of people like them are inferior may affect self-worth and identity development.

Most importantly, culturally specific aesthetic preferences do not develop in a vacuum, independent of other modes of expression. The aesthetic preferences of social interaction, speech, dress, and sound production given cultural priority are unconsciously informed by a single set of psychological principles and assumptions about hierarchy, community, gender, and the dissemination of power.

These principles create a web of interlinked aesthetics. The conservatory operates in an especially powerful aesthetic web because the individual student is highly motivated to meet aesthetic expectations while under intense scrutiny. For anyone who has not been a classical music student, it may be hard to appreciate the intensity of the pressure brought to bear by persistent aesthetic evaluation in a conservatory. Students are judged on their performance and behavior in recitals, studio classes, masterclasses, orchestral sections, and chamber group rehearsals. They are judged on the repertoire they select, what they choose to wear in performance, and how they speak from the stage. In practice spaces, students will judge one another's practice techniques. Students are also judged by how they speak and behave in non-musical social situations, and by their everyday clothing.

It's not too much of a stretch to say that in the highest-caliber, tightly pressurized conservatory environment, everyday life can resemble a constant performance, punctuated by moments of downtime. These pressures are consciously understood by conservatory students, but the undercurrent of race and class in this aesthetic environment is unacknowledged. Students gain social and musical advantage when their self-presentation most closely mirrors a specific set of aesthetic values.

> *My first concert [at school], I came to see the orchestra. And this old lady – I'm sitting in front of her and I just feel a hand in my hair. Not even so much as a "hey, my name is…" You know what I mean? She just touched me. And she was just investigating, but I was like, this is not the time or the place, and honestly, there is no time and there is no place. And I'm like, "ok, ma'am," because you can't get mad. The whole angry Black woman thing – I feel like I was never really allowed to be angry about something.*
>
> (African-American conservatory graduate)

Challenges of self-presentation are perhaps most acute for vocalists. Deeply personal bodily aesthetics become professionally salient, such as hair color and texture, skin color and complexion, and height and body shape. Perception of a singer's race and gender affect our perception of their actual vocal sound quality and timbre. Historical assumptions that vocal quality is innate and determined by physiology, and that physiology is determined by the imaginary category of race, have created assumptions about vocal quality and race and led to the racialization of voice types.

In 1903, a *Washington Post* review hypothesized that the Negro voice featured a "peculiar vibrating quality," caused by folds in the vocal cords of Black singers.[30] In the world of opera, there is not yet a normalized and regular acknowledgment of the racist nature of many opera plots, lyrics, and dialogue; the problematic nature of the ideals and standards of white beauty in relation to specific roles; and negative associations with racial/ethnic groups around which certain roles may have been written. Singers are familiar with the characterization of certain voice types in which, for example, mezzo-sopranos and basses are the villains. But what does it mean for the Black student basso or mezzo-soprano who is continually cast as a villain, in the context of stereotypes about Black criminality and violence? What does it mean for the Latina soprano who is cast in the role of a sexually alluring heroine, in the context of stereotypes about Latina sexuality and the objectification of Latinas in American culture?[31]

> *I remember in a certain opera role, for the character I was playing, people were like, "You need to move your hips. You know how to move your hips, right? Just move your hips! Just do it." And I was like, oh, I feel uncomfortable. I'm not moving my hips for you. Yes, I can move my hips – what are you really asking me to do when you're saying that, though? You know, why tell me to do that in front of everybody?*
>
> (Latina opera singer)

Conclusion

In this chapter, I have introduced the concept of racialized aesthetics, the impact of aesthetic assimilation, and the historical application of music education in service of aesthetic assimilation. I agree that anyone, given desire and training, can learn to appreciate and perform Western classical music. But the assumed supremacy of white aesthetics in Western classical music, and the subordination of other aesthetics and musics, is problematic. The next chapter will explore strategies to understand, oppose, and transform supremacist assumptions in Western classical music.

Notes

1 Katherine Schaeffer, "In A Rising Number of US Counties, Hispanic and black Americans are in the Majority," *Pew Research Center*, November 20, 2019, www.pewresearch.org/fact-tank/2019/11/20/in-a-rising-number-of-u-s-counties-hispanic-and-black-americans-are-the-majority/
2 Jeffrey S. Passel and D'Vera Cohn, "US Population Projections: 2005–2050," *Pew Research Center*, February 11, 2008, www.pewresearch.org/hispanic/2008/02/11/us-population-projections-2005-2050/#:~:text=Racial%20and%20Ethnic%20Groups,compared%20with%2014%25%20in%202005
3 Nicholas Jones, Rachel Marks, Roberto Ramirez, and Merarys Ríos-Vargas, "2020 Census Illuminates Racial and Ethnic Composition of the Country," *US Census*, August 12, 2021, www.census.gov/library/stories/2021/08/improved-race-ethnicity-measures-reveal-united-states-population-much-more-multiracial.html
4 An industry-wide study carried out by the League of American Orchestras in 2014 found that African Americans comprised only 1.8% of orchestral musicians nationwide, while only 2.5% of performers identified as Latinx. "There are real barriers for African American and Latinx musicians entering our profession," said Jesse Rosen, president of the League of American Orchestras, in a 2018 interview with NBC News.
5 For examples, see the Pinkney Foundation, Google's partnership with HBCU career centers, and the Black Squares chess program.
6 Bruno Nettl, *Heartland Excursions: Ethnomusicological Excursions on Schools of Music* (Urbana: University of Illinois Press, 1995), 82.
7 Dylan Robinson, "To All Who Should Be Concerned," *Intersections: Canadian Journal of Music* 39, no. 1 (2019): 139.
8 Zach Ferriday, "White Noise: Classical Music on Stormfront," *VAN Magazine*, January 11, 2018, https://van-magazine.com/mag/white-noise/
9 A later discussion in this chapter mentions the similar belief expressed by white assimilationists in the 19th century–that participation in white educational systems would physically turn the skin of Black people white.
10 Jeremy F. Lane, "Pierre Bourdieu's Forgotten Aesthetic: The Politics and Poetics of Practice," *Paragraph* 27, no. 3 (2004): 82–99.
11 Anna Bull and Christina Scharff, "'McDonald's Music' Versus 'Serious Music': Production and Consumption Practices Help to Reproduce Class Inequality in the Classical Music Profession," *Cultural Sociology* 11, no. 3 (2017): 283.

12 Nettl, *Heartland Excursions*, 34.
13 Anthony Abraham Jack, *The Privileged Poor* (Cambridge, MA: Harvard University Press, 2019), 21.
14 Joe Feagin, *The White Racial Frame: Centuries of Racial Framing and Counter-Framing*, 2nd ed. (New York: Routledge, 2013), 100.
15 Ibram X. Kendi, *Stamped From The Beginning: The Definitive History of Racist Ideas in America* (New York: Nation Books, 2016), 436.
16 Ella Myers, "Beyond the Psychological Wage: Du Bois on White Dominion," *Political Theory* 47, no. 1 (2019): 6.
17 Woodson first launched "Negro History Week" in February 1926, to celebrate the birthdays of Abraham Lincoln and Frederick Douglass.
18 Abigail C. Wilson, "The Role of Music in Assimilation of Students at the Carlisle Indian Industrial School," *The Gettysburg Historical Journal* 18 (2019): 95–97.
19 Smithsonian National Portrait Gallery. "Zitkála-Šá." https://npg.si.edu/object/npg_S_NPG.79.26
20 Kendi, *Stamped From The Beginning*, 127–128.
21 Nina Eidsheim, *The Race of Sound: Listening, Timbre, and Vocality in African American Music* (Durham: Duke University Press, 2019), 40.
22 John M. Kang, "Deconstructing the Ideology of White Aesthetics," *Michigan Journal of Race and Law* 2 (1997): 283.
23 Minh-Ha Pham, "Racial Plagiarism and Fashion," *QED: A Journal in GLBTQ Worldmaking* 4, no. 3 (2017): 67.
24 Kang, "Deconstructing the Ideology of White Aesthetics," 285.
25 Robin James, "Oppression, Privilege, and Aesthetics: The Use of the Aesthetic in Theories of Race, Gender, and Sexuality, and the Role of Race, Gender, and Sexuality in Philosophical Aesthetics," *Philosophy Compass* 8, no. 2 (2013): 104.
26 Brenda Dixon Gottschild, *Waltzing in the Dark: African American Vaudeville and Race Politics in the Swing Era* (New York: St. Martin's Press, 2000), 11.
27 Gottschild, *Waltzing in the Dark*, 12–15.
28 Olly Wilson, "Black Music as an Art Form," *Black Music Research Journal* 3 (1983): 3.
29 My comparison of Wilson and Gottschild is inspired by Paul Taylor's reference of these sources in *Black Is Beautiful: A Philosophy of Black Aesthetics*.
30 Eidsheim, *The Race of Sound*, 69.
31 Michael Cantrell, "Voice Types of Opera Villains: Collaborative Study of Vocal Tessituras of Villains and Heroes in Opera," *Undergraduate Research Journal* 19, no. 8 (2015): 3–5.

Suggested Readings

Eidsheim, Nina S. *The Race of Sound: Listening, Timbre, and Vocality in African American Music*. Durham, NC: Duke University Press, 2019.

Jack, Anthony Abraham. *The Privileged Poor*. Cambridge, MA: Harvard University Press, 2019.

James, Robin. *The Sonic Episteme: Acoustic Resonance, Neoliberalism, and Biopolitics*. Durham, NC: Duke University Press, 2019.

Kendi, Ibram X. *Stamped From The Beginning: The Definitive History of Racist Ideas in America*. New York: Nation Books, 2016.

Morrison, Matthew. "Race, Blacksound, and the (Re)Making of Musicological Discourse." *Journal of the American Musicological Society* 72, no. 3 (2019): 781–823.

Nettl, Bruno. *Heartland Excursions: Ethnomusicological Excursions on Schools of Music*. Urbana, IL: University of Illinois Press, 1995.

2 Transforming the White Racial Frame

Introduction

In the first chapter, I suggested that American conservatory education bears the hallmarks of assimilationist educational programs, and that the effects of this assimilation could be effectively viewed through the lens of aesthetics. This chapter dives deeper into the specific analytical tools and strategies necessary to understand and combat aesthetic supremacy in Western classical music education. It is particularly important to understand the white racial frame and its application to musical aesthetics and pedagogy, and the need for solutions that are transformational rather than additive.

I will attempt to address issues of racial exclusion using specific examples and propose modest solutions in the realms of theory, musicology, and pedagogy.

Reinforcement of Aesthetic Supremacy through the White Racial Frame

Sociologist Joe Feagin coined the term "white racial frame" to describe the invisible mechanism used to reinforce white cultural norms in American institutions, a worldview including not only racial stereotypes but also narrative, emotional responses, and perceptions of spoken language.[1] Although Feagin was exploring generalized bias by whites against people of color, his description highlights the aesthetic dimension of prejudice in its reference to aesthetic characteristics such as imagery, narratives, emotion, and speech.

DOI: 10.4324/9781003217053-3

The white racial frame relies on three central mechanisms to reinforce certain norms. White persons and people of color often tacitly support the reinforcement of these norms because we have all been exposed to implicit social messages supporting white cultural supremacy. The first mechanism is the minimization of racist behavior and ideas, under the assumption that their actual impact should be minimal. After all, why should a stray comment made about someone's hair or skin color affect someone so strongly? The second mechanism, the assumption of white moral virtue, encourages the conclusion (in the absence of evidence) that the bad actor in any report of racist behavior didn't really mean what they said or did, or was misunderstood. This second mechanism facilitates the first by suggesting that a racist comment wasn't really intended in the way it came across, and therefore should have minimal impact. The third mechanism, normalization, suggests that racist behavior is an unavoidable fact of life and must simply be accommodated.

Philip Ewell applies Feagin's ideas to the field of music theory to demonstrate how music theory as a discipline enforces musical preferences aligned with whiteness and maleness. Ewell, pictured in Figure 2.1, proposes that several principles animate music theory's white racial frame:

- That the music and musical theories of white persons are either the best, or the only, framework for analyzing music.
- Specifically, that music and musical theory in historically German-speaking areas, from the time of Johann Sebastian Bach to the early 20th century, are the pinnacle of musical composition and theoretical analysis.
- That race and gender has played no role in the evolution or institutions of music theory and should be off-limits as a discussion topic, because to discuss it would be unfair at best, and racist at worst.
- That the best scholarship in musical analysis is promoted regardless of race.
- Adopting the language of "diversity and inclusion" is sufficient to address any racial issues in the field of music theory.[2]

Music theory's white racial frame is difficult to detect because alternative theories have been excluded from the pedagogical canon. The theoretical basis for the implied harmonies of figured bass and Roman numeral analysis was proposed by the German musician Georg Joseph Vogler in the early 19th century.[3] Undergraduates spend years studying examples of sonata form from music by Wolfgang Amadeus Mozart, Joseph Haydn, and Ludwig van Beethoven. The persistent foregrounding of music and music theories from Germany and Austria has trapped us in a loop of circular logic. The elevation of any piece of Germanic music is rationalized through its alignment with the theories designed specifically to analyze Germanic music.

Music analysis long ago began to move beyond "absolute music" to examine the encoding of identity and narrative structure within formal processes, and the social and political ramifications thereof. Susan McClary and Suzanne Cusick identified the encoding of

Figure 2.1 Philip Ewell.

Photographer: Pascal Perich.

gender and sexuality in formal compositional structures and voicing strategies from the 18th and 19th centuries.[4] McClary and Michael Marissen have identified the encoding of class, particularly social and economic strategies embraced by the bourgeoise, within motivic structures and formal processes in works such as the Brandenburg concerti.[5] This identification aligns with research by Anna Bull and Christina Scharff demonstrating the similarities between modern-day "middle-class" values and Western classical music, including the types of spaces utilized, modes of dress, and practices of listening.[6]

This research suggests that musical elements of the core repertoire studied and performed by conservatory students communicate a particular ideological and political orientation toward class and gender. I would like to examine the encoding of gender in a particular structure, that of sonata form, and propose a racialized interpretation of some of its foundational elements in regard to power, domination, and subjugation.

In the 19th century, musicians were familiar with the alignment of primary and secondary themes with gender conventions. A. B. Marx had labeled the primary theme as "masculine" and the secondary theme as "feminine," owing to the contrast between the typical "heroic" and dynamic impetus of primary themes and the relatively fluid character typical of second themes; Arnold Schoenberg later identified the tonic key as the "patriarchal ruler."[7] In this context, the juxtaposition of two key areas, I and V, takes on a new significance.

If the primary theme is where the composer, and by extension the audience, are to psychologically locate themselves, the narrative implication is perhaps one of traversing a divide, where the "heroic" and "masculine" protagonist travels a great distance to the key of V, where he encounters something beautiful and "feminine," occurring in the key of V. This narrative first act finishes with closing material before the development section. There, the themes encounter surprises and danger in the form of unexpected modulations and motivic fragmentation. Eventually, the primary theme escapes this danger zone and returns to its primary key, bringing a pleasant surprise back home to the key of I with it: the secondary "feminine" theme, appearing in the tonic key itself.

This painfully reductive description of sonata form does not explain many other formal questions, such as the evolution of sonata form from the classical to romantic era, the appearance of the secondary theme in keys other than V, sonata-rondo form, or monothematic expositions. A. B. Marx was possibly inspired by certain sonatas of Beethoven, but not all of Beethoven's sonatas function in this way. Moreover, many sonatas are not by Beethoven. Or perhaps the dominant is only an extension of the tonic-triadic self, and not an oppositional "other" that must be purged or overcome.[8]

But I believe this model captures something essential about the intersectional encoding of nonmusical concepts like gender, protagonism, gratification, and the relationship between linear time and progress. Theoretical controversies notwithstanding, for me, this "rough draft" of sonata form has enough going for it that I present it in Figure 2.2's Highly Reductive Sonata Form Cartoon.

Western classical musicians are taught, above all, that our primary function is to intensify the emotional release of the tonic's confrontation with the dominant, concluding with the ultimate, perfect, authentic, cadential arrival. We're judged by how well we elicit and sustain this tension. And in Western classical music from German-speaking lands in the 18th–19th centuries, tonic confronts dominant over and over, and wins.

A critical element of sonata form is the relationship between I and V on a large scale, but also on a small scale. In four-part writing we learn that in a major key, the tonic goes to the subdominant, which goes to the dominant, and then resolves, usually, back to the tonic. One of the rules we learn is that "V can't go to IV"; once we get to V, it is not permissible to go "backward." But there's plenty of music where V does go to IV, such as, for instance,

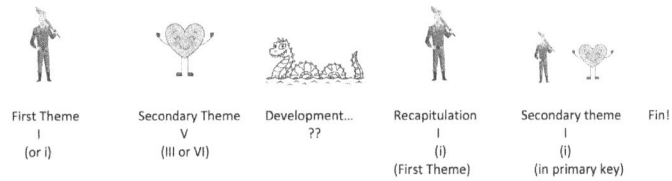

First Theme	Secondary Theme	Development...	Recapitulation	Secondary theme	Fin!
I	V	??	I	I	
(or i)	(III or VI)		(i)	(i)	
			(First Theme)	(in primary key)	

Figure 2.2 Highly Reductive Sonata Form Cartoon.

Artist: Christopher Jenkins.

in the blues. Of course, what does this word "can't" mean? V can go to IV; it does so in non-classical genres all the time. What we mean is *in music of quality and value, V does not go to IV*. This rule has been determined by theorists who have examined "good music" and determined that it doesn't do this. But how do students learn to identify "good music"? They are taught that it is music where V doesn't go to IV. This insistence that movement from V to IV sounds "bad" when it is such a common modern-day technique suggests that some other psychological procedure is operational.

If anything, it should be a little puzzling that when we know how standard classical repertoire is going to conclude that it's destined to cadence on the tonic without fail, we persist in listening through to the end. There's simply no question – we're going to end on the tonic. Yet we still listen, often to the same work repeatedly. We watch Hollywood movies in a similar way; even sometimes in a good movie, one has to think, "why am I watching this? The hero is just going to win." But if it's a good movie, if the tension is sustained, the audience watches because they are living vicariously through the hero and want to know *how* the hero is going to win. Something similar is happening with our relationship to the themes of a standard Western classical symphony. All sorts of values are bound up in our fascination with the V–I resolution: mastery (of I over V), control (over the key we're in), self-assertion, and self-actualization in the process of the theme working itself out through the development. We are proven master of our domain over and over again.

But what if, for some reason, I is unable to confront V? What if the protagonist lacks the social capital or political empowerment to defeat the enemy and demonstrate mastery? What about those whose perpetual historical condition has been to suffer through others' demonstration of mastery over them? What if history has demonstrated that confrontation of V invites physical and psychological torture, death, and annihilation, not only of oneself but of one's community?

To conclude a musical form in a foreign key seems to invite the dissolution of the self. So, when confronted with V, to sustain the ego defenses necessary to prevent psychological fragmentation, the listener may find it imperative to return to the tonic. But if the resources necessary to overcome V are not available, we have to surrender, to retreat, to negotiate and give way. Perhaps this is the sound of V going to IV. It is no wonder that this happens in the blues, in the music of people forced into a physically and psychologically subservient position, in which resistance invites violence. Surrender to V would seem to be the only option. Yet returning to I is a self-affirmation necessary to perpetuate psychological integrity, and requires some type of negotiation with V. In the blues, this negotiation in the context of an unequal power dynamic is often performed ironically, as a slide from V to IV at the end of the twelve-bar blues structure.

The relationship between music and language is helpful in this scenario if music, like language, is a form of communication beyond the absolute. The relationship between marginalized peoples and language should bear a similarity to the relationship with music. Kamalu ya Salaam uses this parallel in discussing the origins of African-American music:

> Let us not overlook an obvious but often overlooked reality: Standard American English (SAE) is not the native language of African Americans...we use English because it was forced upon us by a dominant culture...There are literally no SAE words to describe adequately the social and psychological history of our people. Indeed, SAE is overwhelmingly anti-Black. Just as all languages propose a worldview and value system, SAE (like all other colonial languages) presupposes the domination of people of color by Europeans and the hierarchical subservience of all things African to anything European...being the creative people we are...we created a nonverbal language [music] which expressed our worldly concerns, as well as our spiritual aspirations. More than any other form of communication, "the music" expresses, at the deepest levels, the realities of our existence.[9]

If music reflects "realities of existence," and the sociopolitical realities of different groups are markedly different, then it is only reasonable that different musics serve different psychosocial needs. My theorizing about the nature of the blues progression is purely speculative and I would not propose it as a unifying theory of Black music. However, a 2022 study at Harvard University about the supposed "universality" of music, titled *Universality and Diversity in Human Song*, found that music was "universal" in that it existed in all cultures, but that "the music of a society is not a fixed inventory of cultural behaviors, but rather the product of underlying psychological faculties that make certain kinds of sound feel appropriate to certain social and emotional circumstances."[10] Ewell demonstrates that the white racial frame has informed the construction of the field of music theory. A white European and male frame surrounds European classical music and the psychological referents upon which its forms and progressions draw. This is because the best-known Western classical music is by white European males, pictured in Figure 2.3.

None of this need be an indictment of these composers or their music. This interpretation does not call for anyone's cancellation. We can love and appreciate all of this music while still acknowledging its foundations. But if this music requires that it be elevated over all others and relies upon psychological referents that are not entirely our own, then to what extent has our personal commitment to this music compromised our own psychological integrity?

Countering White Supremacy: Fugitive Pedagogy and Culturally Responsive Pedagogy

The term "fugitive pedagogy" describes the Black resistance against the violently assimilationist character of the educational system mandated by all-white school boards during Reconstruction in the South. Black teachers in all-Black southern schools would actually bring two sets of lesson plans to the classroom, one hidden, and one visible: a white-approved (and racist) curriculum on the desk, and a Black-positive lesson plan hidden in their laps.[11] Inspired by Carter Woodson, for whom aesthetic elements were a principal component of the resistance against assimilationist education, fugitive pedagogy reserved a particular role for music. This was illustrated by the performance of certain musical works only in the absence of white supervisors in schools.

Woodson, who initiated Black History Month (originally titled "Negro History Week") in 1926, wrote extensively on assimilationist education in *The Miseducation of the Negro*, and emphasized the role of aesthetics in preserving a psychologically healthy environment for Black children.[12] Woodson partnered with Black teachers to develop new standards and principles not

Figure 2.3 Photo of a typical poster of white, male, European composers as found in American music schools; photo by the author wearing a Black Lives Matter T-shirt.

Photographer: Christopher Jenkins.

just for how classrooms should operate, but the literal and symbolic appearance and feel of the classroom, so as to reorient the student's aesthetic experience. As Jarvis Givens writes, "Woodson and the teachers he partnered with operated from a belief that transforming the symbolic order of schools was an integral part of transforming the world in which they lived."[13] Carter's pedagogy touched on many aesthetic areas, such as:

- Symbolic belonging through visual and aural official representations of the institution.
- Presenting stories about Black people with whom students could racially and politically identify through a culturally resonant storytelling modality.
- Humanizing Black perspectives to counter antiblack values.

- Taking opportunities to critique the master narrative as it is reified through content and attitudinally.

Givens quotes John Bracey, a student in a school employing Woodson's pedagogy, as describing Woodson's impact as "atmospheric," a reference to the power of his pedagogical aesthetic. Bracey gives a striking musical example of fugitive pedagogy:

> In homeroom every morning – you had to do as part of your culture, you sang the Negro national anthem…We only sang "The Star Spangled Banner" when white people showed up… you had to go to the assembly hall the day before and practice "The Star Spangled Banner" because nobody knew it. If you said national anthem…we stood up and sang "Lift Every Voice and Sing." If you had wanted to bet money with me when I was in fourth grade, I would have told you "Lift Every Voice and Sing" was the national anthem. White people had some crap they sang, but this is the national anthem.[14]

An inexact but meaningful corollary to fugitive pedagogy still exists today in conservatories: the covert efforts of students to study and participate in the performance of styles of music outside of the Western canon, when this activity is sometimes forbidden by classical instrumental studio professors. For example, some teachers may forbid their classical voice performance students from enrolling in jazz lessons or a gospel choir group, but those students may keep it a secret that they have found a gospel church group or jazz ensemble in which to sing near campus. Or, a classical piano student who has been told to focus their practicing on etudes and fundamentals might pay for improvisation lessons outside of school or from another student. It should not be surprising for white readers to know that students of color also receive covert advice from faculty and advisors of color.

Take a moment to place these ideas in context. Musicians, and artists more broadly, are challenged to see the world from a unique vantage point and share that with the world. Every acclaimed musician, regardless of genre, time period, or cultural context, shares a single attribute: a unique voice. Too often, music schools encourage the pursuit of a narrow strand of excellence that precludes the development of a unique voice and promotes uniformity. That narrow strand of excellence is racially delimited, and restricts access to creativity's prerequisite: curiosity. How will we foster one-of-a-kind artists when we occupy their time with pursuits of sameness?

Culturally Responsive Pedagogy and the Deficit Model

Culturally Responsive Pedagogy (CRP), also known as Culturally Responsive Teaching (CRT), is underutilized in conservatory education. Gloria Ladson-Billings articulated the theory of CRP in the 1990s in proposing that academic achievement is affected by the resonance of curricular material with students' cultural backgrounds. CRP is intended to be an empowering pedagogy that supports students intellectually, socially, emotionally, and politically through cultural references.[15] It rests on three pillars: academic achievement, cultural competence, and sociopolitical awareness.[16] This sociopolitical awareness empowers students to challenge inequities in school and in the work environments they enter.[17] Constance McKoy and Vicki R. Lind's *Culturally Responsive Teaching in Music Education: From Understanding to Application* provides many useful examples of culturally responsive practices in music education, and emphasizes the importance of designing music instruction in the absence of music literacy.[18]

CRP requires the rejection of cultural deficit theory in favor of cultural difference theory. Cultural deficit theory holds that the underperformance of students of color should be attributed to deficiencies in their home cultures. Cultural difference theory holds that student achievement can be significantly impacted by differences between home and school cultures. In other words, the deficiency is not on the student's side; it is the institution that is deficient if it has not made sufficient effort to narrow the gap between its cultural values and the values of its students. Aesthetics are relevant to culturally responsive music education because declarations of ideal sonic beauty are culturally limited. Supremacist thinking demands that "alternative" theories of beauty be discarded as inferior, while student musicians of color simply require proper training to help them understand "true" beauty.

Cultural deficit theory is often represented in evaluations of the academic and musical abilities of African-American and Latinx students when professors assume that some of these students need to be taught "how to behave" in a range of areas, from stage presence to appropriate engagement in studio class and the private lesson, aside from their education about what constitutes objectively "beautiful" sound production and intonation. Tyrone Howard and Clarence Terry include the rejection of a cultural deficit ideology in their articulation of CRP's key principles, which they believe also include combatting the normalization of Eurocentric and white middle-class forms of discourse and culture, a political commitment to supporting equity and challenging injustice, recognizing the complexity of culture, and exhibiting a culturally informed concept of care for students' academic and personal well-being.[19]

Making Progress Transformative, Not Additive

These culturally responsive elements should be transformative, rather than additive. For example, it is not sufficient to simply include several compositions by Black composers in addition to the standard material covered in a music theory course. The analytical and pedagogical approach should be transformed to fit a diverse student population. Diversity conversations in Western classical music have tended toward additive change because it is far easier to add to an existing repertoire of pedagogical behaviors or music, to start doing new things that come easily, than to change or stop doing what one is accustomed to doing.

For example, some orchestras now program works composed by people of color and women, in addition to the classics. In conservatories, new positions have been added to help students of color, and orchestras have added minority fellowship positions. The problem with Western classical music is that it has been *conceptually* exclusionary, not just *functionally* exclusionary. An additive approach toward "fixing" racism – to add more people of color and their music – does not address the deeper conceptual issues that require transformation.

The additive orientation toward diversity is evident in music history textbook entries for artists like William Grant Still, pictured in Figure 2.4. If the first edition of *A History of Western Music*, published in 1960, mentions Still or his music anywhere, I could not find it.[20] While one might be tempted to believe this omission was merely a reflection of the book's focus on music of

Transforming the White Racial Frame   39

the renaissance, baroque, and classical periods of European music, this edition mentions other modern American composers and includes a section on works with "folksy" or "vernacular" themes, such as George Gershwin's *Rhapsody in Blue*, Roy Harris' *Folk Song Symphony* (described as a combination of "Negro spirituals and cowboy tunes"), and compositions by Robert Palmer, Walter Piston, Roger Sessions, and Howard Hanson. Still was born in 1895 and had been composing for decades before the publication of this textbook. His well-known Symphony No. 1 "Afro-American," was premiered in 1931, and he composed several operas after receiving a Guggenheim Fellowship in 1934. The first edition of *A History of Western Music*, in which he does not appear, was published 26 years later.

In the third and fourth editions of *A History of Western Music*, published in 1980 and 1988 respectively, Still is mentioned in one sentence.[21,22] The seventh edition, published in 2006, devotes two paragraphs to Still.[23] The discussion of his music is limited to its impact on other African-American composers, and is much shorter than entries about his white counterparts. For example, a discussion of the music of Ruth Crawford Seeger takes up several pages and mentions she was the first woman to win a Guggenheim Fellowship in music.[24] While this is an excellent and important reference, especially given the historical marginalization of female composers, Still's Guggenheim prize is not even mentioned in his entry. The ninth edition of *A History of Western Music*, published in 2014, provides the same two paragraphs about Still, largely unchanged.[25] If any readers wonder if the relative obscuring of Still is an anomaly, George Walker, the first African-American to receive a Pulitzer Prize for music, also does not appear in the ninth edition.

Why would Still not have been featured in the first edition of *A History of Western Music*? An obvious reason would be the historical bias against the promotion of composers who are not white men. Clara Schumann, for example, does not have her own sentence in that first edition either; she shares one with a male composer. This bias is compounded by the additive evolution of textbooks and the absence of a transformation of the organization and framing of previous editions. A composer who is mentioned in a single sentence in a first edition may receive three sentences in the next edition, and a whole paragraph in the next. But this

Figure 2.4 Portrait of William Grant Still, circa 1949. Van Vechten (Carl) Collection, Library of Congress.

Photographer: Carl Van Vechten.

additive approach preserves the bias reflected in the initial effort. Between the first edition and subsequent publications, Still goes from no mentions to several sentences, while the lesser-known white American composer Roy Harris goes from several sentences to several paragraphs.

Students who go through standard conservatory training read these textbooks at a formative stage in their academic development and are told that the textbook preserves an objective hierarchy of importance, rather than a point of view. When those students conduct research and write their own books, what is to stop them from following the same lines of inquiry and replicating the same hierarchy? In order to change the expression of bias in past representations, music scholarship must be transformative, rather than additive. The theory of culturally responsive pedagogy supports this point. Ewell argues a similar point when he mentions that the inclusion of examples by Black composers in conventional music theory textbooks is an insufficient measure of diversity, and that adding musical examples by Black composers to theory textbooks does not address the real problem: that western tonality functions as the central organizing principle recognized in music theory's scholarship and pedagogy, to the exclusion of other musics and aesthetics.[26]

Any effort to diversify will be less effective if it only involves additions to existing content, such as a new position, repertoire, or a course. Examples of transformation would involve revamping curriculum, not simply to include diverse works but to deemphasize skills such as four-part and fugue writing, and analysis of keyboard sonatas by Joseph Haydn and Wolfgang Amadeus Mozart. Also, changing audition requirements to replace standard works with works by composers of color, devising new courses of study in previously marginalized areas, and allowing ensembles or courses outside the Western canon to satisfy core requirements could greatly enrich our music curricula.

The case of George Frideric Handel is illustrative. Handel spent much of his career in London, becoming a naturalized British citizen and accepting opera commissions from the Royal Academy of Music. It was through many financial investments that Handel was able to cover losses on opera seasons so as to support himself and remain in London, where he was able to write many of his most famous works. The source of these investments, however, is problematic. Handel was a principal investor in the Royal African Company and the South Sea Company, two of the largest slave-trading companies at the time.

The veracity of this claim has been demonstrated by the discovery of Handel's signature on various logs for sale of stock.[27] In a music history course designed for a diverse student body, perhaps we should view Handel's story through this prism rather than simply adding this fact to Handel's general narrative. Does the story of Handel change? Perhaps it does if we reconsider that he depicted the liberation of man through the acts of the son of God – as in the *Messiah* – while he personally and professionally benefitted from enslavement. Did Handel consider this irony or reflect upon the significance of his investment? What does it mean for African-American churches to celebrate the work of a man who was financially committed to the enslavement of Black Africans?

Some professionals still raise questions as to why this type of information should be relevant. Shouldn't we judge artists solely by the musical content of their work and leave out racial moralizing and judgment? David Hunter has an eloquent answer:

> Just as the artifacts of slavery and its profits persist into the 21st century – shackles, cargo lists, inventories, houses, paintings – so too does its auditory trace. The 18th century will never "be over" as long as we continue to perform and study and hear its music. In this light the unwillingness of writers heretofore to acknowledge – let alone address – slavery's funding of work creation, performance, and attendance can at best be described as neglectful; at worst it is a continuation of institutionalized racism by exclusionary means. Music history cannot of itself right the wrongs of slavery, but it can and should be open about the roles and actions of the participants who used the profits from owning people and subjugating them for personal or business profit to fund lifestyles in which music played a prominent role.[28]

Centering race in musicology requires an acknowledgment that race has always been central to questions of musical analysis and quality, that music is inherently political, and as such can be neither absolute nor universal.

Conclusion

Music theory's white racial frame is a microcosm of the conservatory's generalized white racial frame. Music students are encouraged to develop a "discriminating" musical taste that excludes anything "popular" and elevates most things Germanic (to dislike Bach, for example, as some students actually do, is a sin), to perfect a particular ideal of sound production, intonation, and diction (in the case of singers), and to master a certain aesthetic of physical and verbal self-presentation in performance. Circular logic justifies the definition of "excellence" as mastery of these areas: How do we know when our sound concept, phrasing, and style of performance are ideal? When they make for an ideal sonic and visual presentation of music that has been defined as "the best." How do we know if a certain piece of music is one of "the best"? When it adheres to analytical frameworks derived from Germanic music of the eighteenth and nineteenth centuries, and our sound concept, phrasing, and style of performance make it sound ideal.

Musical alterity, even when encouraged or tolerated, is usually defined as inferiority. This kind of thinking reinforces itself and encourages those who have been "successfully" trained in Western classical music to eagerly export these aesthetics to other communities and countries. Or, as Ewell puts it, "The fact that many of the ideas from functional tonality appear in so many of the world's musics is a direct result of the power of colonialism and hegemony."[29]

The effects of the white racial frame do not receive enough attention in music theory, musicology, and pedagogy. Culturally responsive pedagogy has been particularly underutilized in higher education in general and certainly in conservatories. An understanding of these theories alone is not sufficient to effect change. Leadership, faculty, and personnel must be properly aligned. The next chapter addresses considerations of staffing and administrative strategies to further institutional change.

Notes

1 Joe Feagin, *The White Racial Frame: Centuries of Racial Framing and Counter-Framing*, 2nd ed. (New York: Routledge, 2013).
2 Philip Ewell, "Music Theory and the White Racial Frame," *Music Theory Online* 26, no. 2 (September 2020): 2.4. https://mtosmt.org/issues/mto.20.26.2/mto.20.26.2.ewell.pdf
3 Floyd K. Grave, "Abbé Vogler and the Study of Fugue," *Music Theory Spectrum* 1 (Spring 1979): 47.
4 Susan McClary, "Narrative Agendas in Absolute Music: Identity and Difference in Brahms' Third Symphony," in *Musicology and Difference: Gender and Sexuality in Music Scholarship*, ed. Ruth A. Solie (Berkeley, CA: University of California Press, 1993), 332–333; Suzanne G. Cusick, "Feminist Theory, Music Theory, and the Mind/Body Problem," *Perspectives of New Music* 32, no. 1 (Winter 1994): 10.
5 Susan McClary, "The Blasphemy of Talking Politics During a Bach Year," in *Music and Society: The Politics of Performance, Composition, and Reception*, ed. Richard Leppert and Susan McClary (New York: Cambridge University Press, 1987), 23–26; Michael Marissen, *The Social and Religious Designs of J.S. Bach's Brandenburg Concertos* (Princeton, NJ: Princeton University Press, 1995), 25–27.

6 Anna Bull and Christina Scharff, "'McDonald's Music' Versus 'Serious Music': How Production and Consumption Practices Help to Reproduce Class Inequality in the Classical Music Profession," *Cultural Sociology* 11, no. 3 (July 2017): 289–293.

7 James Hepokowski, "Masculine–Feminine: Are Current Readings of Sonata Form In Terms of a 'Masculine' and 'Feminine' Dichotomy Exaggerated?" *The Musical Times* 135, no. 1818 (August 1994): 494–499.

8 Hepokowski, "Masculine–Feminine," 497.

9 Kalamu ya Salaam, "It Didn't Jes Grew: The Social and Aesthetic Significance of African American Music," *African American Review* 29, no. 2 (Summer 1995): 352.

10 Helena Asprou, "Music is a Universal Language, New Harvard University Study Proves," *Classic FM*, January 9, 2020, www.classicfm.com/music-news/study-proves-music-is-universal-language/

11 Jarvis R. Givens, *Fugitive Pedagogy: Carter G. Woodson and the Art of Black Teaching* (Cambridge, MA: Harvard University Press, 2021), 1.

12 Carter G. Woodson, *The Mis-Education of the Negro* (Trenton, NJ: Africa World Press, 1998), 64.

13 Givens, *Fugitive Pedagogy: Carter G. Woodson and the Art of Black Teaching,* 204.

14 Givens, *Fugitive Pedagogy: Carter G. Woodson and the Art of Black Teaching,* 209.

15 Gloria Ladson-Billings, *The Dreamkeepers: Successful Teaching for African-American Students* (San Francisco: Jossey-Bass, 1994), 17–18.

16 Gloria Ladson-Billings, "Toward a Theory of Culturally Relevant Pedagogy," *American Educational Research Journal* 32, no. 3 (Autumn 1995): 469.

17 It could be that the historical conservatism of Western classical music education contributes to the reluctance to embrace CRP in conservatories, because the sociopolitical awareness it requires would empower conservatory students to challenge inequities and abuses of power in the conservatory system.

18 Vicki R. Lind and Constance McKoy, *Culturally Responsive Teaching in Music Education: From Understanding to Application* (New York: Routledge, 2016), 45.

19 Tyrone C. Howard and Clarence L. Terry, Sr. "Culturally-Responsive Pedagogy for African American Students: Promising Programs and Practices for Enhanced Academic Performance," *Teaching Education* 22, no. 4 (2011): 347–348.

20 Donald J. Grout, *A History of Western Music* (1st ed.) (New York: W.W. Norton and Company, 1960).

21 Donald J. Grout and Claude Palisca, *A History of Western Music* (3rd ed.) (New York: W. W. Norton and Company, 1980), 699.

22 Donald J. Grout and Claude Palisca, *A History of Western Music* (4th ed.) (New York: W. W. Norton and Company, 1988), 825.
23 J. Peter Burkholder, Donald J. Grout, and Claude Palisca, *A History of Western Music* (7th ed.) (New York: W. W. Norton and Company, 2006), 889–890.
24 Burkholder, Grout, and Palisca, *A History of Western Music*, 885–886.
25 J. Peter Burkholder, Donald J. Grout, and Claude Palisca, *A History of Western Music* (9th ed.) (New York: W. W. Norton and Company, 2006), 900.
26 Ewell, "Music Theory and the White Racial Frame," 5.
27 David Hunter, "Handel and the Royal African Company," *Musicology Now*, June 14, 2015, https://musicologynow.org/handel-and-the-royal-african-company/
28 Hunter, "Handel and the Royal African Company."
29 Ewell, "Music Theory and the White Racial Frame," 5.

Suggested Readings

Ewell, Philip. "Music Theory and the White Racial Frame," *Music Theory Online* 26, no. 2 (September 2020): 1–29. https://mtosmt.org/issues/mto.20.26.2/mto.20.26.2.ewell.pdf

Feagin, Joe. *The White Racial Frame: Centuries of Racial Framing and Counter-Framing*, 2nd. ed. New York: Routledge, 2013.

Givens, Jarvis R. *Fugitive Pedagogy: Carter G. Woodson and the Art of Black Teaching*. Cambridge, MA: Harvard University Press, 2021.

Hunter, David. *The Lives of George Frideric Handel*. Woodbridge: Boydell & Brewer, 2015.

Ladson-Billings, Gloria. *The Dreamkeepers: Successful Teaching for African-American Students*. San Francisco, CA: Jossey-Bass, 1994.

McClary, Susan. *Feminine Endings: Music, Gender, and Sexuality*. Minneapolis: University of Minnesota Press, 2002.

Woodson, Carter G. *The Mis-Education of the Negro*. Penguin Classics, 2023.

3 Concrete Advice for Leadership and Staff

Introduction

Previous chapters provided theoretical background for understanding and opposing the assimilationist character of Western classical music education. In this chapter, I provide specific recommendations for inclusive practices in conservatories. Staffing is indeed important because access is not the same thing as support. Schools such as Oberlin Conservatory, New England Conservatory, and a few other predominantly white conservatories that existed at the turn of the 20th century have historically offered access to people of color and female-identifying students. Many of those students have reported feeling unsupported, and have experienced discrimination.

Over the past few years, many conservatories have added staff positions dedicated to DEI work. On the individual level, such positions can be effective. Other schools have chosen to create positions that oversee a DEI center, sometimes in addition to working with students on the individual level. Owing to a recent proliferation of national institutions committed to supporting African-American and Latinx student musicians, institutional partnerships have also become popular, although they can be expensive. It is not certain, however, that these initiatives can generally be effective in ameliorating the effects of the larger hostile climate for students of color.[1]

In general, should schools of Western classical music create dedicated DEI positions? I would suggest that the answer is yes. Students of color face a range of challenges that can be addressed to some extent by a dedicated staff member. This type of position

DOI: 10.4324/9781003217053-4

can be very helpful, on the individual level, for those specific students with whom that individual is able to forge connections. The presence of a "DEI center" in a music school can be at least reassuring to students of color and normalizes an institutional DEI commitment, which is important internal messaging for faculty and staff.

Individual students can also benefit from the opportunities provided by partnerships with national organizations (although assuring the value of funding and efficacy of external programming is critical in insuring that every dollar in the "diversity budget" is well spent). The value of personal mentorship, cultural understanding, academic assistance, and financial, emotional, and social support should not be underestimated in improving the student experience and aiding retention.

These positions, centers, and partnerships are helpful but limited. Crucially, they cannot be expected to create deep, meaningful, and long-lasting institutional change on their own. They must operate in tandem with concerted efforts by faculty and administration to change core curricular content and musical programming. Otherwise, students of color may get enough support to survive and to graduate, but they will not be able to fully thrive as people or musicians.

When students perceive that a school environment is hostile, they may have experienced microaggressions or had outwardly racist interactions with members of the campus community. Black students in predominantly white institutions regularly report experiencing "racial/ethnic hostility, inequitable treatment, microaggressions, isolation, tokenization, lack of representation, and overt racism" that "diminish sense of belonging and institutional commitment."[2] These issues are reported or experienced on the individual level but are systemic. There may also be proximate causes located in student life or campus culture. Even if students do not perceive an environment to be hostile, they may struggle to adapt socially, academically, or financially. Staff positions can be empowered to address some of these issues and provide various types of support by mediating conflicts, creating new student life programming, connecting students to resources, and providing emotional and cultural connection. DEI centers can offer training, sponsor guest speakers, and provide diverse extracurricular content.

But my experience has been that at root, the institutional expression of core values is the main problem. Historically, those values have aligned with supremacist thinking that elevates white European art forms. The expression of white supremacist core values gives license to students, faculty, and staff whose own values align with white supremacy to engage in micro–and macro-aggressions. Because the core purpose of a teaching institution is to teach, core values and aesthetics are generated mostly from one place: musical choices in the curriculum.

What we teach and how we teach it creates a ripple effect reverberating far beyond the classroom. We communicate a particular set of musical and social aesthetics when music theory and history curricula focus on European art music; when inflexible gender binary dress codes, consisting of historically European costuming, are enforced for concert dress; when large ensembles historically have limited programming to music by composers of a certain race and gender; when vocal students are taught that there is one "correct" pronunciation of English; or when the study of Western classical music topics is required for students focused on African-American music but not vice-versa. These musical and social aesthetics include rigidity, inflexibility, enforcement of hierarchy by gender, class, and race, and a tacit understanding of the superiority of whiteness. A position, center, and/or partnership cannot substantively address these systemic issues.

Leaders of institutions that have created these positions and/or centers should be commended because they have committed substantial funds and energy to improve the climate, and they at least recognize there is a problem. But the danger in creating a DEI position focused on student support or a DEI center is that it may reduce pressure to take further action on the curriculum. This is not to say that such positions can't be deeply valuable for students, or facilitate deeper discussions in the future. But if curricular efforts are not happening in tandem, the short-term results are likely to be superficial. The bottom line is that musical and pedagogical choices in conservatories reflect a supremacist value system. The only way to generate an inclusive environment is to make different musical and pedagogical choices. DEI positions will be most effective when they are able to support individual students and are also positioned to partner with faculty and executive leadership to create change in the curriculum, musical programming, and degree programs.

An alternative approach is to prioritize the hiring of faculty members from diverse backgrounds, rather than inaugurate new positions, centers, or potentially expensive partnerships. This solution can be very effective, but it depends on who is hired, and into what type of position. First, those faculty must be hired into tenured, tenure-track, or non-contingent positions so they are on equal footing. Second, the solution is not merely to hire faculty members who of a certain color, but those who will foster a new set of core values through their teaching and programming.

There is no guarantee that any given faculty member of color will share a commitment to diverse musical values. Finding, hiring, promoting, and retaining the right faculty member is tricky for many reasons. Graduate schools tend to inculcate traditional values through their training and weed out those who think differently; faculty on search committees tend to replicate themselves when hiring; and the rare candidates who make it through this gauntlet are highly competitive on the market and likely to feel alienated and alone once they are hired. In schools with tenure, retaining these faculty through the tenure and promotion process is difficult if other faculty do not consider their work valuable or know how to evaluate it.

The most effective way to shift core institutional values is to operate at multiple internal levels simultaneously because the effects are mutually self-reinforcing. Creating staff positions, recruiting new faculty, educating board members, and helping faculty better understand curriculum diversification create momentum when they occur in parallel. A great danger is that efforts to diversify will devolve into a box-checking exercise, one of many agenda items at a board meeting. Creating a new staff position or organizational partnership provides an all-too-easy answer to the question "What is your school doing about diversity?" It should not be possible to deliver a genuine answer to this question as a 30-second elevator pitch. Real answers are deep, complex, and will probably generate considerable internal controversy.

There are many obstacles to conservatory diversification, two of which I would like to articulate. One is that the diversity question – What does it mean to diversify Western classical music? – too easily becomes a problem in need of a solution: How does our institution solve the diversity problem so that we can move on to other issues? Ta-Nehisi Coates labels this line of thinking "solutionism": the idea that solutions are always available, even to complex problems of historical and systemic injustice.[3] Solutionism, as an iconic American concept, is firmly rooted in traditional white American views of the world. There is a close relationship between solutionism and American political economy. The very concept of democratic elections is presaged on the promise of solutions. Consulting firms are built upon the promise of solutions. A founding myth of the U.S. is that any problem can be solved, and that we solve our own problems through the focused effort (call it "gumption") of those who are intelligent and competent. (The corollary is that communities suffering from long-term systemic issues are assumed to be responsible for their own problems.)

Solutionism in racial issues is particularly destructive because it allows people to ignore the extent to which racism is so thoroughly baked into existing systems that it cannot be uprooted. It is critical to understand how systems have been built and have evolved around a mold of racist ideas so that they cannot be deracialized; new systems may be necessary. Solutionism helps individuals avoid the shame and guilt of acknowledging one's own complicity in the effects of structural racism.

The lack of diversity in Western classical music education is a problem without a clear solution. This is exactly what we should expect of any complex issue. Racism and injustice in the criminal justice system are multifaceted problems without a clear solution, as are redlining in housing and implicit biases. The lack of diversity in STEM fields, PhD programs, and Western classical music are complex, multifaceted problems requiring education to unpack them and sophisticated efforts to address them. There is no point in the near future in which any American conservatory should expect to have become sufficiently "diverse," if only because American society will continue to change and evolve.

Another issue is the conflation of diversity, and difference, with mediocrity. Studies have demonstrated that diversity improves organizational performance in various ways, and team excellence is not possible without diversity. But we do a disservice to the cause of diversification when its importance is communicated primarily through simple platitudes like "diversity is excellence." It's not that simple, because "excellence," like "truth," or "beauty," is culturally defined and delimited. Diversification must go beyond demography and enter into the deconstruction of supremacist thinking and a transformation of core values.

There are some gatekeepers who will cede overt opposition to diversity initiatives but retain supremacist modes of thinking, a phenomenon I label *"diversity capitulation."* They do so to excuse themselves from a critical examination of their own values while going through the motions of a hollow, performative obeisance to "diversity" as they view it. Capitulation, defined as "to cease one's opposition," is insufficient when what's needed is the courage to learn and grow by challenging one's own values.

Diversity capitulation happens when, for example, a reluctant department chair agrees to hire an additional faculty member who specializes in non-Western music, but keeps those courses out of the core requirements. It happens when a search committee member for a studio position feels pressured to hire a Black candidate who specializes in music they view as substandard, but then covertly discourages their colleagues from inviting that new hire to take part in faculty concerts or social events. Diversity capitulation occurs when individuals holding racist attitudes grudgingly accept what they interpret as pressure to give special treatment to minorities, but then covertly mistreat people of color.[4]

Diversity capitulation is a serious challenge to diversity efforts because it is largely unseen. It can be negated through a focus on more specific, accurate, and influential diversity goals. For instance, the primary goal in hiring African-American faculty members should be to have ever-growing numbers of African-American faculty members feel supported by their deans and colleagues and engaged by the larger campus community, not simply to have them on the website. The primary goal in hiring more specialists in non-Western musics should be to find ways of gradually moving that content into core requirements, not simply to offer it as an add-on.

In general, the forces opposing aesthetic and curricular diversification in Western classical music are far too great in scope to be addressed through the addition of a single staff position. This doesn't mean that adding a staff position will not enhance feelings of well-being and retention for students of color; doing so could be extraordinarily meaningful. A best practice would be to do so in conjunction with other major changes, and to give this position a meaningful role in determining the content and scope of those changes. As mentioned in the first chapter, Dylan Robinson's open letter "To All Who Should Be Concerned" lists issues to address, such as altering admissions requirements that privilege Western music performance and the music of white European males; changing the makeup and approach of academic courses, rather than simply adding token content; ending the tradition of white male leadership in administration and tenured faculty; and connecting with local communities of color.[5]

Below is a summary of what one might consider when writing a position description:

- **Identify discrete roles and do not overload the position with incompatible responsibilities.** If the person hired into a student-support or center-directing role is expected to work one-on-one with students, support student groups, lead a DEI committee, facilitate faculty trainings, run programming, teach courses, and work with admissions and recruitment, it is unlikely they will be able to do all of those things excellently. An extensive portfolio suggests that one's institution has so much diversity work to do – and most institutions do – that one position will be insufficient. If needs have been identified in all of these areas, perhaps it is necessary to hire more than one person.

    It is challenging to teach while working in an administrative position, and yet these candidates will, hopefully, teach more diverse courses. Teaching also can lend the position a degree of legitimacy among the faculty if an official teaching post is appended to the position. But if a teaching load is required, other duties must be supported so that teaching can be done at a high level.

- **If the position is intended to "lead" on diversity issues, empower it to work with faculty and administration to facilitate curricular change.**

    Faculty must retain control over the curriculum, but if there aren't curricular changes, the issues that make a DEI position necessary will never be addressed. Leaders need to articulate a vision for what they want these positions to achieve and to prepare faculty to think about what curricular diversity will mean in their area.

- **Consider hires with DEI-specific experience, rather than hires with musical experience and no DEI background.** Conservatories, as predominantly white institutions (PWIs), are comfortable hiring minority candidates with musical training and whom already subscribe to the basic mission, vision, and values of the typical conservatory. The assumption is that these candidates already "understand what we do" in the conservatory, code for the implicit understanding that they have already been ideologically trained and unconsciously conditioned to accept supremacist aspects of conservatory training. Candidates without musical training but experience in DEI, social justice initiatives, and arts education may be less competitive. But one of the primary functions of these positions is to work transformatively within DEI. One might conclude that what's desired is less transformation and more maintaining the status quo.

  Musical training is important, but a candidate without a music degree might also be successful. A master's degree and relevant work experience in DEI should be required. Search committees may mistake teaching or administrative experience with minority populations for actual DEI experience. Helpful DEI experience, or training for the inexperienced, includes theoretical training and experience in organizational theories of change, theories of diversity, teaching about principles of culturally responsive pedagogy, and management theories of higher education.

Here are several suggestions to be considered by indivduals hired into these positions:

- **Implement a Longitudinal Climate Survey.**

Data provides concrete information and effective presentation of data (sometimes) compels action. It's easier to ignore anecdotal accounts of bias than to dismiss a report detailing that a certain percentage of students feel they have experienced harassment or discrimination.

Climate surveys involve the collection of longitudinal data from faculty, staff, and students to portray the average experience and highlight outliers. They are useful, necessary, and/or legally obligatory after reports of long-standing pattern of misconduct. Ideally, climate surveys will:

- Collect information regarding frequency and type of bias incidents
- Determine if a pattern of misconduct exists in a given area of study
- Determine if a pattern of misconduct is linked to a particular individual or individuals
- Provide a description of the operating culture in a given area (faculty, student, or staff culture may differ greatly)
- Be conducted by a team of outside legal professionals
- Closely involve HR, legal counsel, and senior leadership
- Pair a wide net for information collection with a specific plan for information dissemination

Many legal firms specializing in higher education law and climate surveys can assist. While it may be tempting to cut corners by surveying with conventional tools available online, the combustible and private nature of this information makes this inadvisable. An external legal firm is well-positioned to exert control over critical issues such as data storage and analysis. The cost of a comprehensive climate survey conducted by an external firm with legal expertise could be far less than the legal and reputational cost of lawsuits related to discrimination, harassment, and/or assault and the poorly managed collection and dissemination of data and documentation.

- **Ally with student leaders and seek out the most vulnerable students.**

It is important to attend student recitals and student-centered/student-organized talks, invite student leaders to meet one-on-one frequently, and sponsor student organizations and attend their meetings, if and when appropriate. When students want to create new organizations, they may face opposition from the administration. It is in everyone's interest to support new student organizations focused on racial, social, and/or economic justice and to work productively with them rather than to nurture a dynamic of opposition.

At the same time, the students in greatest need of emotional and financial support are the least likely to seek it out, perhaps because they are unaccustomed to being helped. A mandate for these jobs should be to serve the most marginalized and vulnerable students.

- **Invest in relationships with individual faculty members, and connect with other campus groups for support.**

If a conservatory has created a position intended to support students of color or lead programs devoted to DEI, it is a sure bet that students have been advocating for greater support for some time. It is also a sure bet that there are some faculty, staff, and students who are opposed to such a position.

Anyone in a "diversity" position at an institution committed to the preservation of European art forms will eventually find themselves in conflict with institutional power centers. By that point, the person in such a position must have already positioned themselves to draw support from allies.

Students may expect these positions to enforce wholesale curricular change overnight. The reality is far more complicated. Tenured/long-term faculty members are invaluable allies because they are the only subject-matter experts with the knowledge base required to make curricular changes.. Staff members can effectively advocate for long-term change by cultivating relationships with individual faculty members.

- **Seek out training and present at conferences.**

An incredibly wide range of skills is required for success in this type of position. New research and scholarship are produced at a brisk pace and the theoretical understanding of the racial politics of Western classical music is evolving rapidly. Incumbents should not feel constrained in pursuing training about best practices. Networking at conferences with members of your field is also essential to bring in fresh ideas and maintain mental health. Staff in these positions should receive professional development funds so they may continue to present professional work at conferences and receive leadership training.

- **Prioritize intersectionality.**

The general expectation of these jobs is that they are intended to ambiguously "support students of color." The needs of a low-income African-American student who is experiencing housing insecurity are very different from the needs of a middle-income Latinx student who does not identify as cisgender and is experiencing gender-based discrimination. These students require totally different resource pools and approaches. Communication styles need to be tailored to personality, which intersects with but is not determined by race, ethnicity, and culture. Student needs vary based on instrument group as well! All of these distinctions must be taken into account when designing student support programs.

Curricular Suggestions

I am not an expert in music theory or musicology pedagogy. But, I can offer a few possible solutions in diversifying curriculum based on examples of successful changes that have made an impact on students.

- **Diversify musical examples and de-emphasize four-part chorale harmonization.**
  I do believe it is still important for Western classical music students to understand the voice-leading rules of counterpoint and the harmonic strategies of Bach's chorales. I also believe that that these students should be able to execute a basic harmonic analysis – even if just by ear – of musical pieces from the baroque, classical, and romantic eras. A problem arises when the development of these skills dominates training to the point of excluding study of musics that do not adhere strictly to these rules. Examples from pop, rap, and R&B musical styles can be integrated into existing curriculum. It is increasingly likely that, if they are successful as performers, students will be asked to perform in at least one of these styles at some point. Harmonic and melodic skills are also often prioritized to the detriment of rhythmic sensibility, which is relatively undeveloped in Western classical musicians. A more diverse range of styles requires a greater emphasis on rhythmic skills.

- **Include genres outside of Western classical music in music theory and musicology courses.**
American conservatory departments have historically characterized music from Afrodiasporic genres as belonging in the areas of jazz, popular music, or ethnomusicology – even though jazz is uniquely American and, arguably, the "true" American classical music. Courses that examine the history and analysis of rap music, R&B, and jazz should be integrated into academic conservatory departments offering core requirements, which are usually music theory and musicology.

   When these courses are included, they can also be focused on specific areas rather than being survey courses. For example, music departments may offer specific courses on Joseph Haydn's piano sonatas or Wolfgang Amadeus Mozart's string quartets, and then a survey course of "world" music. The (un)availability of relevant faculty may make it challenging to offer multiple courses on, for example, Indian classical music, but the creation of courses about more specific styles or traditions (South v. North India, for example) communicates that this music is also worthy of concentrated and focused study.

- **Allow core requirements to be satisfied by a range of electives rather than a fixed curriculum.**
There would seem to be two choices: one is to continue to require a "great books" version of conservatory training that emphasizes historically canonical works. This approach supposedly guarantees that every student graduates with a knowledge of, at least, the greatest hits of Ludwig van Beethoven, Johannes Brahms, Johann Sebastian Bach, and Wolfgang Amadeus Mozart. (It is no secret that for some students, this examination is cursory, and their resulting knowledge is superficial.)

   Or, students can pick from a various range of electives offering a deep dive into diverse genres including music that may not strictly adhere to conventional rules of harmony. The second approach is a better fit for a more diverse conservatory population. It is possible to adopt this approach and still ensure students have basic and core analytical skills by retaining some core courses, and integrating some basic and core training into subsequent electives.

- **Allow performance electives to be satisfied by a more diverse range of ensembles and performance experiences.**
  As more schools offer ensemble experiences that involve "non-traditional" music, those ensembles can be integrated into the core curriculum. (Over the past five years, Oberlin has inaugurated a gospel choir, a course on the history and analysis of rap music, and a djembe orchestra class. Students can satisfy major requirements with these courses.) Given that professional freelancers are now often called to perform music from an enormous variety of styles, Western classical players should be able to satisfy at least some of their requirements by playing in non-Western ensembles.
- **Encourage or compel students to take courses in improvisation and/or composition as a "creative requirement."**
  Each student has an incredible opportunity to develop their own unique voice, the character of which is determined by unique personality, but also intersects with culture and is thereby put into relationship with race and ethnicity. Providing students with creative skills they can leverage to communicate that uniqueness should be an essential component of any musical training, but especially in music schools intending to matriculate an increasingly diverse student population.
- **Diversify the repertoire required for entrance auditions and the repertoire performed by students and faculty.**
  This suggestion seems so obvious that it is hardly worth mentioning. I do so because even though many schools have begun this process, it is not always approached in a substantive way that will ensure long-term change. It is entirely possible for at least 50% or more of the repertoire presented by faculty and student ensembles in a semester to be written by composers of color and/or who identify as female.

  Entrance requirements can be similarly changed; but it is important that if entrance requirements become more diverse, that departments encourage students to study and perform diverse repertoire as well. It should not be that, for example, the single time a student learns a work by an African-American composer is for their entrance audition.

- **Offer new concentrations and degree programs that work synergistically with the creation of new courses in diverse areas.**
An advantage of creating new minors, concentrations, or even majors that integrate "diverse" performance styles is that if they are popular, they will demonstrate the potential of these areas of study and incentivize the creation of new courses, or the reorientation of old courses to be credited toward new areas of study. For example, in 2021, Oberlin's faculty voted to approve an African-American Music Minor, leveraging Oberlin College's Department of Africana Studies and Oberlin Conservatory's courses focused on African-American music.

An Additional Note for Students

It is difficult for students to accept that the timeline for meaningful change may place it beyond the horizon of their graduation date. The irony is that students have a tremendous amount of power to demand change, but are not always able to understand the power of advocating for changes that will not materially affect them. It is important for students to reflect upon the effect of their advocacy and activism on the circumstances of students far in the future.

Some changes will last in perpetuity and/or be harder to erase, such as:

- Changes to syllabi and curriculum
- New courses (that not only teach about music by composers who are not white male Europeans, but explore oppressive structures within Western classical music)
- New degree programs, including minors or concentrations
- The endowment of new student support funds

While some diversity initiatives are stymied by opposition, many things don't happen because of a sheer lack of imagination and energy. Students have both. These are the ingredients necessary to cut through the sclerotic inertia that often characterizes decision-making in higher education.

Conclusion

The suggestions in this chapter are by no means exhaustive, and are limited by my own experiences and viewpoint. Hopefully, they offer something useful to leadership, students, faculty, and incumbents of positions intended to support students of color and potential candidates for those positions.

One topic that has not been explored thus far is the importance of equity. Its proper application in official policy is extremely important for the academic progress of disadvantaged students, but "equity" as a term is frequently ill-defined and misunderstood. The next chapter will discuss the pursuit of equity in conservatory education and addresses strategies for special populations, including those with intersectional identities.

Notes

1 Positions intended to implicitly support students of color may or may not be legal, depending on the funding sources and location of your institution. It is important to consult state and federal law closely when crafting position descriptions.
2 Chyrstal A. George Mwangi, Barbara Thelamour, Ijeoma Ezeofor, and Ashley Carpenter, "'Black Elephant in the Room: Black Students Contextualizing Campus Racial Climate Within U.S. Racial Climate," *Journal of College Student Development* 59, no. 4 (2018): 457.
3 Ta-Nehisi Coates, *Between the World and Me* (New York: Spiegel & Grau, 2015).
4 I do not mean to suggest that I witnessed these specific examples at Oberlin; these are hypothetical examples that do reflect some real-world experiences.
5 Dylan Robinson, "To All Who Should Be Concerned," *Intersections: Canadian Journal of Music* 39, no. 1 (2019): 137–144.

Suggested Readings

Ahmed, Sara. *On Being Included: Racism and Diversity in Institutional Life*. North Carolina: Duke University Press, 2012.

Ewell, Philip. "Music Theory and the White Racial Frame." *Music Theory Online* 26, no. 2 (September 2020): 1–29. https://mtosmt.org/issues/mto.20.26.2/mto.20.26.2.ewell.pdf

Kajikawa, Loren. "The Possessive Investment in Classical Music: Confronting Legacies of White Supremacy in U.S. Schools and

Departments of Music" in Kimberlé Williams Crenshaw, Luke Charles Harris, Daniel Martinez HoSang, and George Lipsitz, eds., *Seeing Race Again: Countering Colorblindness Across the Disciplines*. Berkeley and Los Angeles: University of California Press, 2019, 155–174.

McClary, Susan. "Narrative Agendas in 'Absolute Music'" in Ruth Solie, ed., *Musicology and Difference: Gender and Sexuality in Music Scholarship*. Berkeley and Los Angeles: University of California Press, 1993, 326–344.

McKoy, Constance. L. and Lind, Vicki R., *Culturally Responsive Teaching in Music Education: From Understanding to Application*. Routledge: New York, NY, 2016.

Robinson, Dylan. "To All Who Should Be Concerned." *Intersections: Canadian Journal of Music* 39, no. 1 (2019): 137–144.

4 Equity

Introduction

In this chapter, I argue that a socially just conservatory will implement policy-level equity provisions for students. Equity calls for all under-resourced students to be provided with what they need to succeed. I discuss needs specific to low-income students, LGBTQ+ students, and disabled students. I would encourage administrators to listen to the students at their institution to learn more about their needs, and to seek out further consultation and training.

I specifically discuss issues affecting transgender students because members of this group may have particular needs in a conservatory setting (especially vocalists), and these needs are frequently misunderstood or mischaracterized. Beyond the moral imperative to meet the needs of these students, it is important to understand that cisgenderism, heteronormativity, transphobia, homophobia, and misogyny are interconnected. Therefore, it is in everyone's interest for conservatories to support students of all gender identities.

Defining Equity

"Equity" is a persistently misused term. It is often cited as a reason why a particular student can't receive a specific type of support not immediately available to others: "It wouldn't be fair – for the sake of equity, we have to treat everyone the same. That means offering everyone the same support." This definition is the exact opposite of equity. The National Association for Colleges and Employers defines "equity" as distinct from equality; equity recognizes that

Equity 63

we all start from different places, and that an ongoing system of rebalancing is required to overcome barriers created by systemic bias.[1] Equity is truly "fair" because it allocates resources differently for individual students, with the intention of giving everyone a more equal opportunity to succeed. Equity practices address the injustice of income disparity, the history of discriminatory treatment of individuals who identify as BIPOC, LGBTQ+, those who are neurodivergent, and those with physical, sensory, or mental disabilities.

Crucially, equity does not require that certain services or departments work only for particular student groups. The same services should be offered to everyone, but everyone should not be treated identically in the application of those services; priority should be given to those who need them most. Crucially, equitable treatment is not predicated on membership in a certain group, but on the particular needs of each individual student.[2]

True equity practices often generate pushback and criticism that equity is unfair because it treats people unequally. The pushback against equity is predicated on an unwillingness to acknowledge the extent to which "unfairness" is baked into our economic, political, and judicial systems, through which students' identities have already been formed by the time they enter college. Students who are not competing on a level playing field are still expected to meet identical standards of "excellence." In a conservatory, underachievement is usually presumed to indicate a lack of musical

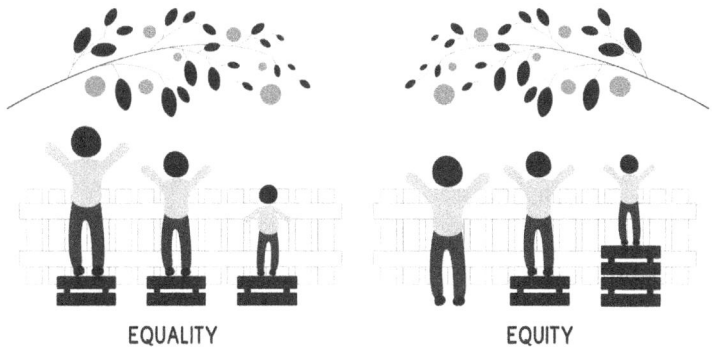

Figure 4.1 Equity v. Equality. Credit: iam2mai.

skill, effort, or commitment. A conservatory's offer of admission means that a student's demonstrated ability, record, and "talent" suggests the potential to succeed, given the right training from the faculty and investment of hard work by the student. It should also represent an institutional commitment to equity by providing each student with the resources they need to succeed.

It is difficult or impossible to recalibrate performance expectations because there cannot be radically different standards for the tempo at which one plays a concerto, how many pieces are performed on a recital, or how in tune one's scales are at a jury, if students are to be prepared to compete at a professional level. But conservatories still do not often account for the fact that students come from vastly different life circumstances and cannot be expected to achieve at the same level if they all receive an equal allotment of resources and are treated identically by policy. There are ways to devise different support systems for students without subverting performance standards or discriminating based on protected categories. Support should be individually tailored based on individual situations and needs.

I just needed somebody to take me under their wing and explain things. I mean, nobody ever taught me how to go to college, nobody taught me how to write a formal paper...or how to use MLA or Chicago style or anything like that. I just needed people to teach me that, even just very briefly.
(Latina conservatory graduate)

As a point of emphasis: equitable policies do not and should not require discrimination in the distribution of funds on the basis of protected categories such as race, ethnicity, religion, sexual orientation, or gender identity. In the educational context, equity applies first and foremost to income, disability, and mental and physical health.[3] Equity does not mean that all students identifying as African American, or as transgender, for example, receive resources withheld from students in other categories. The whole point of equity is that it targets the specific need of each individual student. Identity categories are suggestive of possible needs, but are not determinative.

Intersectionality, or the overlapping of multiple identity categories such as race, class, gender, and sexual orientation, is really the animating concept behind equitable targeted support. Needs are not dictated by membership in one category or another. This is why it is so important to identify the specific needs of any given student.

Psychological Factors Affecting Music Performance

When external circumstances affect the performance of marginalized students, their teachers may attribute that negative outcome to a student's personal weakness or deficiency. In fact, scientific findings demonstrate that whites tend to attribute negative outcomes for and behaviors of Blacks to internal characteristics, and positive outcomes and behaviors to external forces, but they do the opposite for whites.[4] This distortion, known as attribution bias, is significant in conservatories, because there are so many occasions in which students are judged, as mentioned in earlier chapters.

The well-documented phenomenon of stereotype threat suggests that in a context where a negative stereotype exists for one's group, fear and anxiety of confirming that stereotype actually elicits underperformance.[5] Marginalized students may underperform in studio class because of their anxiety in playing for a mostly-white group of students, or underperform in auditions or juries before mostly-white faculty groups, or be afraid of speaking up or vocalizing in music theory or aural skills classes, or develop a negative attitude toward these classes and discount content that appears Eurocentric. These phenomena support the argument above for equitably resourcing students.

An important element of equity is attitude – a willingness to try to understand a student's circumstances, how their background may influence their performance, and what they need to succeed, rather than judging every student by the same inflexible standard in the absence of a personal relationship or understanding. That inflexible standard undoubtedly exists in professional-level competitions and orchestral auditions, and there is obviously a compelling argument for replicating that tension in juries and recitals. An "equity attitude" is appropriate for those who have taken on the responsibility of supporting students in their journey toward becoming the best musician they can be. For faculty members, there need be no tension between adopting an "equity attitude" in providing what students need to succeed, and judging them objectively in arenas where that type of judgment is precisely what they need. There also should be no tension between an "equity attitude" and accepting that ultimately, some students will simply not succeed as music performers. The attitude shift consists of understanding that some students are less likely to succeed if everyone receives the same support.

Adopting an "equity attitude" is an important first step toward establishing an institutional culture of equity. At the very least, it is ideal to not expel students if the policies suggested by an equity attitude might result in their retention. An "equity attitude" is suggested by the following example.

The conservatory spring recital season is full of stress and celebration. Families travel across the country to attend. To cater the post-recital reception, some parents drive to the local grocery store or bring desserts from home. Families with greater resources will offer a fully catered buffet or even hire a licensed bartender to serve drinks.

I recall when an extremely talented and popular low-income student was preparing for his graduation recital. This student's family members were unable to travel for the concert or send funds to pay for a reception. His friends cooked and transported food to the hall.

This student asked if he could use an office minifridge to store food before the reception. The response he received was "We can only do it for you if we're going to do it for every student. It wouldn't be fair otherwise."

It seems logical to say that it would not be fair to offer this service to only one student. A written policy governing student use of the office minifridge would probably say something like this. But it's curious how easily the word "fair" creates barriers between students and what they need to succeed. In this case, an equity approach would suggest that for low-income students, the use of that fridge has much more value than for others.

Is it really true that a student could have no one in their family to support them at this critical moment? Shouldn't the student just have to figure this out like everyone else? Consider the extent to which many American families are disconnected from support taken for granted by the middle and upper classes. Not every student, or members of their family, will always have regular access to a bank account, have a credit card, have a driver's license or Federal ID, have a working cell phone or internet access, or time off from work, paid or unpaid. Some students have no living family members upon whom they can rely.

> *So, I took my first lesson with her. And she said to me "You are going to be big. You have so much potential. I haven't heard a voice like yours in years, and I need to work with you." Nobody had ever said those words to me before. My mom couldn't really afford lessons. And it cost 30 bucks a lesson. That was a lot for my mom. I remember the teacher said, "Don't worry, don't pay me for this lesson." And she was also low income, my teacher, you know, so it was a lot for her to say, "Don't pay me," because she needed the money as well.*
>
> (Latina conservatory graduate)

Catering is the least of a low-income music student's concerns. Summer festivals span multiple months, and because participation adds up to several additional semesters of training, those who cannot attend are at a significant disadvantage. Instrument purchase and maintenance costs are enormous. It's pretty daunting for a conservatory to even attempt to provide all of these funds, but it may be possible to provide funds for smaller-cost items and to distribute them in an equitable fashion. If possible, consider other data in addition to Expected Family Contribution (EFC), which may not fully reflect a student's actual need. Parents may also adjust their level of financial support outside of tuition due to a shift in student's self-declared identity (LGBTQ+, transgender/nonbinary, or change in religious beliefs) that can lead to financial insecurity not reflected in the EFC. Funds particularly appropriate for low-income students would be:

- **Summer support funds.** Four years of attendance at summer music festivals represents an entire year or more of instrumental instruction unavailable to low-income students, who often cannot afford that tuition and usually need to work during the summer. Unpaid internships are often not possible for low-income students. An argument can be made that conservatories have a moral obligation to subsidize summer experiences for low-income students.

- **Emergency/short-term expense funds.** Seemingly insignificant emergency costs can derail low-income students. These costs include replacement strings, reeds, or shipping for an oversize instrument. News articles have mentioned students who withdrew from school because they could not afford a $25 bus ticket to and from campus.[6] More students struggle to afford a $250 oversize baggage fee for their instrument.
- **Travel costs** for auditions and application fees are significant stressors. Consider also whether students have access to working computers with appropriate software (compositional and otherwise) for their courses.

There was this program at [local community music school], where you could audition and get [subsidized] lessons. But the maximum scholarship you could get was 25% of the cost of the lesson. And so, I was like, y'all gonna be at 75%? If I have to pay 75%, you might as well [ask for] all of it. I literally don't have it.
(African-American conservatory graduate)

Another suggestion for equity is to make policies and fee structures more flexible. It is common to put a registration hold on the accounts of students with unpaid balances, a group in which students of color are often overrepresented. But the consequences can be significant; these students end up unable to select courses they need and may be shuffled into the least desirable sections, times, and/or professors, where they have a lower chance of success. Greater flexibility around fees and holds is the easiest step for most institutions to take. It is also equitable to make application and other fees income-sensitive.

It seems necessary to offer targeted support to low-income and first-generation (LI-FG) students (with the caveat that, especially in a small school, students in these categories may not want to be singled out or identified in any public way). Many liberal arts schools offer targeted support specifically for LI-FG students, but this is less common in conservatories. Because of life stressors and financial uncertainty, students in this group are more likely to have particular needs in terms of financial and emotional support, and Latinx and African-American students are statistically more likely to be LI-FG. Student support staff should be trained on best practices for supporting this student population and, in a small conservatory environment, admissions staff and student support staff can communicate about the status of incoming students.

BIPOC and LGBTQ+ student support groups can also be very helpful, whether student-led or institution-driven. In conservatories, student groups organized around specific types of music and musicians, such as the Oberlin College Black Musicians Guild (OCBMG), help students support one another and enhance musical diversity. Peer cohorts, upper-class mentorship, and alumni mentorship programs can also be effective in helping these students succeed.

On Issues Facing Transgender Performers

Because the transgender experience is frequently misunderstood, it is important to develop a shared vocabulary. Below is a short list of basic definitions adapted from *The Singing Teacher's Guide to Transgender Voices:*[7]

Gender: Behaviors, emotional traits, and social expectations associated with being male or female. Gender is a societal construct that varies across cultures and time periods.

Gender Expression: Presentation of gender through manner and appearance; may be but is not necessarily related to gender identity. Is not simply binary; exists on a spectrum, including an androgynous self-presentation.

Gender Identity: An individual and personally held feeling of being a man, woman, both, neither, or other nonbinary identity. Each person's gender identity may be distinct from the outward expression of identity or perception of others.[8]

Cisgender: A person whose gender identity is congruent with their gender as assigned at birth.

Transgender: A person whose gender identity is incongruent with their gender as assigned at birth. It is an adjective ("that person is transgender") and **not** a noun ("those transgenders").

Misgender: To misidentify a person's gender intentionally or unintentionally, by using incorrect names, pronouns, or statements about an individual based on one's perception of their gender.

The Singing Teacher's Guide to Transgender Voices is a useful resource that covers subjects ranging from singing with chest binding and other body-shaping garments to the effects of hormone therapy on the voice and body, and post-transition considerations for pitch and register. The Musicians Health Collective also offers policy suggestions.[9]

Even with the recent popular exposure of transgender celebrities and American TV shows normalizing transgender identity, transgender and nonbinary people are still consistently subject to dehumanization in American society. Consistent use of pronouns is one of the easiest ways for faculty and staff to reinforce a culture of inclusivity. The most common pronouns in use as of 2023 are they/them, she/her, and he/him, and these are easily integrated into personal introductions (e.g., "My name is _____, I use [the pronouns] she/her.").

Sometimes people who otherwise appear well-intentioned in their treatment of marginalized groups, or who are members of marginalized groups themselves, mock the use of pronouns. The use of pronouns by cisgender people implicitly acknowledges the humanity of a group that has been profoundly structurally disempowered. By doing so, cisgender people relinquish structural power. Relinquishing structural power is a moral imperative but can also be challenging, even for those who are disempowered themselves.

In a conversation with an acquaintance who learned that I worked at a progressive college, she exclaimed while laughing "Isn't that where you have to use your pronouns all the time, and you can't use the term 'guys' or the students will jump all over you? Oh my god, I could never do that!" Ironically, this person was an educator who vigorously advocated for more diversity training and equity work at their institution and thought of themselves as an ally for students of color. These sentiments are not uncommon, and translate to "I am not fully comfortable embracing the legitimacy of transgender identity and giving up the privilege I hold over this group."

Unsurprisingly, transgender performers report that their careers have been limited by discrimination. The pianist Sara Davis Buechner won bronze at the 1986 Tchaikovsky competition and performed with the New York Philharmonic and Philadelphia Orchestra, but found that after coming out as transgender, she was no longer booked by major orchestras and could not be hired by universities.[10] Transgender vocalists face special barriers to acceptance by peers, teachers, and industry. Xavia Publius, a transgender vocal performer, characterizes the assignment of voice parts as a heteronormative mode of behavior regulation in which singers with lower voices are assumed to be heterosexual cisgender men, while those with higher voices are assumed to be heterosexual cisgender women.[11] (Sexual orientation is thus also presumed to align with stereotypical assumptions as well.)

Gender-neutral teaching requires an overhaul of the heteronormative conceptual framing influencing musical interpretation and pedagogy. The addressing of voice types as "men," "gentlemen," "women," and "ladies," rather than the actual voice part being sung, reflects gender preconceptions. On the practical level, small ensemble coaches and studio teachers should learn students' pronouns and avoid misgendering, which can create tension between teachers and students. But on the conceptual level, musicians should also interrogate our tendency to employ heteronormative, gendered, and sexualized language to describe musical concepts and sound quality.

Name Changes

Transgender students should have the option to change their name in institutional records, insofar as is legally allowable, and keeping in mind they may not have had an opportunity to change their legal name before attending school. It can be traumatic to be forced to use or repeatedly be referred to by a "dead name," that is, the birth name of a transgender person who uses a new name as part of their gender transition.

The process of changing one's legal name varies by state and is usually time-intensive, but institutions can make it easier to change one's name on institutional records. Especially in conservatories, students' names appear constantly on ensemble rosters and programs, not to mention their diploma. Procedures can be instituted to ensure that students' preferred names are used in these instances (including on their diploma). Even though registrars will retain a record of a student's dead name if it is their legal name, it is ideal for students to not usually see or hear that name while at school.

Professors and Pronouns

The easiest way to feel certain of a student's preferred name and pronouns is to arrange regular opportunities for students to indicate them. At the first small ensemble, studio, or academic class meeting of each academic year, for example, a professor can model pronoun use and ask everyone to introduce themselves with their pronouns. (Administrative leadership can also set a standard by using pronouns in their own introductions.)

In large ensembles, students can be asked to supply their preferred names and pronouns via an online form or similar method. In initial class meetings, it is a good practice to avoid first names by calling roll using last names only, and then asking students to state their preferred first names and pronouns. Consistent misgendering, even if it is completely unintentional, will generate friction in the teacher–student relationship, and even with other students who merely witness it happening. Persistent misgendering that is clearly intentional should be viewed as discriminatory behavior and investigated according to institutional policies regarding discrimination and harassment. Below are a number of additional suggestions:

Are Gendered Addresses Used when Speaking to Ensemble Sections? In Voice and Aural Skills Classes, Are Professors Encouraged to Refer to Students by Voice Type and Not Gender?
It is common for choral conductors and ear training instructors to address voice sections as "ladies…" or "gentlemen…" and orchestral conductors may address sections as "guys…" But although it might feel like a heavy lift, it is actually pretty easy to do away entirely with gender when addressing groups. Voice types and names of sections can be employed instead. It's ideal to avoid gendered language used in addressing members of large ensembles because it is not practical to know the gender identification of every member of the group.

Do Large Ensembles Enforce Gendered Dress Codes?
It is typical to designate one style of dress for "ladies" and another for "gentlemen," tacitly reinforcing a heteronormative gender binary. A single dress code that works for everyone might be ideal – "concert black," for example – and dress codes should omit moralizing injunctions such as "modest" or "appropriate,"

as these rely upon cisgendered and heteronormative notions of sexual/social propriety. If only two separate types of dress are deemed acceptable – and there are aesthetic and cultural arguments for expanding upon the standard European dress – then simply describe the two types of acceptable dress, leaving it to students to determine which they prefer without referencing gender.

Are All-gender Bathrooms Widely Available and Properly Equipped?
The availability of comfortable bathrooms and dressing rooms is critical for musicians, since we spend so much time in them preparing to go on stage. If retaining several gender-specific bathrooms is a concern, it can be possible to convert some restrooms into all-gender or gender-neutral bathrooms, which should be single-person use or have separate stalls. Consider installing all-gender dressing rooms, which would also contain separate stalls for each individual. Also consider installing dispensers and receptacles for sanitary/hygiene products in all bathrooms and dressing rooms for all genders.

On Neurodiversity, Disability, and Mental Health

Some may feel that disability accommodations are less relevant in music programs because standard academic accommodations, such as extra time on a test or access to note-taking services, are not applicable to music performance. While it is certainly true that extra time to perform a concerto is not a possible accommodation, conservatories often underestimate the volume of students with undiagnosed issues requiring accommodations or other support.

When music students are dismissed from an institution, it is often because they have not succeeded in academic courses even if they are musically proficient. Some of these students can be retained with targeted academic support and assessment services. Executive functioning tutors might be even more helpful at conservatories than in liberal arts colleges, given the challenge of organizing one's time around endless hours of practice plus rehearsal and academics.

Conservatories may also underestimate the musical capabilities of students with major disabilities or discount the existence of effective accommodations that can help them succeed. Students with complete vision impairment, for example, are fully capable of becoming professional musicians, as is demonstrated by the *Al Nour Wal Amal* orchestra, an Egyptian ensemble of limited-vision female musicians.

Physical accessibility of performance and rehearsal spaces remains one of the biggest issues in the performing arts. Old construction and poor design can make it impossible to navigate these spaces in a wheelchair. Newer spaces may be better designed but might fail to clearly include Braille lettering on every sign. Because people who are not disabled can miss details that seem small but are critically important, it's essential that a staff member is clearly identified for reports of inaccessibility by disabled students, faculty, and staff. It's also ideal that these reports are acted upon in a timely manner and that the responsible staff member follows up with the reporting individual to ensure that the changes made meet their needs.

Even though students are under intense pressure for long periods of time, mental health needs in a conservatory are often overlooked. Besides the pressures of consistent evaluation by others, the extensive hours students spend alone in practice rooms while engaging in intense self-criticism are not conducive to mental health. High levels of stress, unreliable income streams, poor sleep habits due to inconsistent working hours, and the potential for substance abuse create a toxic landscape for the mental health of musicians generally, not to mention young students.

The fact that these issues affect professionals should be a clue that earlier intervention is necessary. Because stigma around discussing any kind of personal weakness is a major issue for conservatory students, it is important to normalize discussions about mental health by communicating clear institutional support and educating studio faculty about the need for student support.

As a final note, although the stereotype of the "brilliant but unstable" creative musician has long been sold in popular culture through movies such as *Amadeus*, the intersection of actual neurodiversity and music performance is just beginning to be explored. Composer Zygmund de Somogyi, who has autism, writes in the blog *I Care If You Listen* about experiences with executive dysfunction in music school, and almost being expelled after feeling too overwhelmed to attend classes.[12] Many well-known artists, such as Solange Knowles, Adam Levine, and Justin Timberlake, have Attention-Deficit Hyperactive Disorder

(ADHD).[13] So many famous musicians have been diagnosed with ADHD that scientists have labelled the gene associated with this condition, *DRD-R7*, the "rock star gene." Many famous musicians have been diagnosed with dyslexia.[14]

Conservatories should do more to help students with similar diagnoses succeed in their coursework. A lack of acknowledgment and support is counterintuitive and counterproductive to the interests of the conservatory, given that academic work can be the biggest stumbling block for a neurodiverse student who might otherwise be incredibly creative and musically successful. Universal Music UK has also produced a handbook titled *Creative Differences: A Handbook for Embracing Neurodiversity In the Creative Industries*, inspired by its CEO's recognition of the contributions of neurodiverse individuals to the company. It includes an introduction by Florence Welch, who has dyslexia and dyspraxia.[15]

Conclusion

Equity is a critical part of the student support discussion because it fulfills the socially just imperative of focusing efforts on students who most need it. Ideally, conservatory staff and faculty with an interest in supporting equitable initiatives will pursue further education and training to stay up-to-date with best practices and contemporary framings. In conservatory education, the conversation around LGBTQ+ identity, neurodiversity, disability, low-income, first-generation students, and issues of marginalization is in its infancy.

Notes

1 National Association of Colleges and Employers, "Equity," *NACE*, www.naceweb.org/about-us/equity-definition/
2 National Association of Colleges and Employers, "NACE's Diversity, Equity, and Inclusion Statement," *NACE*, www.naceweb.org/about-us/naces-diversity-equity-and-inclusion-statement/
3 These identities intersect with other protected categories in important ways. African Americans are twice as likely as whites to live in poverty; Latinx people are 1.5 times as likely. Young adults who identify as LGBTQ experience homelessness at 120% the rate of heterosexual cisgender youth. 50% of Black and Latinx transgender youth experience depression.

4 José M. Causadias, Joseph A. Vitriol, and Annabelle L. Atkin, "The Cultural (Mis)attribution Bias in Developmental Psychology in the United States," *Journal of Applied Developmental Psychology* 59 (2018): 65.

5 Claude Steele and Joshua Aaronson, "Stereotype Threat and the Intellectual Test Performance of African Americans," *Journal of Personality and Social Psychology* 69, no. 5 (1995): 797.

6 Karen Weese, "When A Sudden, Small Expense Threatens an Entire College Career," *The Washington Post*, January 30, 2022, www.washingtonpost.com/education/2022/01/30/college-poverty-expense-cost-dropout/

7 Liz Jackson Hearns, and Brian Kremer, *The Singing Teacher's Guide to Transgender Voices* (San Diego, CA: Plural Publishing, 2018), 10–19.

8 Gender identity and gender expression are distinct from sexual orientation, which is the gender expression to which one feels sexually attracted.

9 Musicians' Health Collective, "Addressing Transphobia and Inclusion in Classical Music: Part 1," *Musicians' Health Collective*, November 23, 2020, www.musicianshealthcollective.com/blog/2020/11/22/addressing-transphobia-and-inclusion-in-classical-music

10 Sara Davis Buechner, "An Evolving Country Begins to Accept Sara, Once David," *The New York Times*, February 3, 2013, www.nytimes.com/2013/02/04/booming/growing-acceptance-for-the-transgendered.html?pagewanted=all.

11 Xavia A. Publius, "Suggestions for Gender Inclusion in Classical Music: A Mini-Cycle," (M.A. Thesis, University of Northern Iowa, 2015), 6–7.

12 Zygmund de Somogyi, "The Autistic Experience and Navigating the Contemporary Music Industry," *I Care If You Listen*, December 15, 2021, https://icareifyoulisten.com/2021/12/autistic-experience-navigating-contemporary-music-industry-casting-light-8/

13 Sam Bowman, "Neurodiversity in Music: Embracing Creative Differences," *Music Think Tank*, February 22, 2022, www.musicthinktank.com/blog/neurodiversity-in-music-embracing-creative-differences.html

14 Tim Ingham, "Are Music Companies Hiring Enough People Who Think Differently?" *Rolling Stone*, January 23, 2020, www.rollingstone.com/music/music-features/music-industry-neurodiversity-941115/

15 Universal Music, "*Creative Differences: A Handbook for Embracing Neurodiversity in the Creative Industries,*" 2020, Universal Music, https://umusic.co.uk/Creative-Differences-Handbook.pdf.

Suggested Readings

Crenshaw, Kimberlé. *On Intersectionality: Essential Writings.* New York, NY: The New Press, 2017.

Hearns, Liz J., and Brian Kremer, *The Singing Teacher's Guide to Transgender Voices.* San Diego, CA: Plural Publishing, 2018.

Hess, Juliet. *Music Education for Social Change: Constructing an Activist Music Education.* New York, NY: Routledge, 2019.

Publius, Xavia A. "Suggestions for Gender Inclusion in Classical Music: A Mini-Cycle." M.A. Thesis, University of Northern Iowa, 2015.

Talbot, Brent C., ed. *Marginalized Voices in Music Education.* New York, NY: Routledge, 2017.

Universal Music UK, *Creative Differences: A Handbook for Embracing Neurodiversity in the Creative Industries.* Universal Music, 2020.

5 Interviews with Young Professionals

This chapter contains excerpts from interviews with Black and Latinx musicians. Some interviewees had graduated recently, while others were further removed from graduation and were working professionally. To retain anonymity for interviewees, some identifying information has been redacted, including information such as instrument played, school attended, and geographic location. Interviews have also been edited for clarity and length.

The experience of being nurtured by adults with personal, emotional connections to Western classical music was viewed by many interviewees as critical in the development of their own connection to music. Interviewees frequently described the early impact of a seminal teaching figure or exposure to Western classical music in the household (often both) as determinative in their pursuit of a musical career. That teaching figure was often described as a truly extraordinary person with a commitment to student success and social justice. (That individual did not always share the student's racial identity.)

It was often through these mentoring relationships that students began to establish their identities as Western classical musicians. These relationships, even if they were relatively brief – seem to have been important, if not essential, catalysts. While the level of parental involvement varied, all interviewees reported that their parent(s) supported their child's musical development and had a positive view of musical training.

The distinction between the types of students characterized by Anthony Abraham Jack as "privileged poor," and "doubly disadvantaged" is felt in these interviews in terms of cultural

DOI: 10.4324/9781003217053-6

capital as currency, measured through experience with Western classical music in home life, and the felt entitlement/right to participation in white American "high" culture. The fact that some students straddle the boundary is an important reminder that experiences exist on a spectrum and cannot be neatly categorized.

> *When people say that, it makes it sound like I really know what I'm doing. But it feels like I'm fighting and clawing my way through, it doesn't feel like this was an inspirational story.*

African-American, Instrumental Player, Recent Graduate

This interviewee identified as an African-American cisgender female. She had earned a bachelor of music degree and had one of the highest GPAs in her class. At the time of the interview, she was receiving instrumental lessons abroad as part of a prestigious competitive fellowship.

Q: Could you talk about your personal and musical background prior to attending school, and how you got involved in playing [your instrument]?

A: This is always the weirdest story because a lot of people say, "I heard [my instrument] and it sounded so beautiful!" Honestly, I couldn't have told an oboe from an elbow. But I had really bad asthma as a kid, and my mom told me that I had to play a wind or brass instrument because it would help. And we had a marching band [at my school] but I didn't want to carry anything heavy. So, I saw the instruments and said, where are the smaller ones? There was [primary instrument] and I was like, yeah, we'll do that.

I was so terrible, honestly. But of course, I would have been because, like I said, I had really bad asthma. I was just really just trying my hardest, but it was not working out.

But once, I went to a different school to help another band. I was in [a town near my hometown] and we just had regular little band classes. I enjoyed it, feeling like I finally could make some notes happen. And eventually, I ended up playing my first little solo for our Christmas concert.

I thought I was really doing something big. Like, I've figured out how to play! I think it was Silent Night. I figured it out by ear because I don't know how I could have even gone about finding the music. I went to my band director, and I said, can I do this? He was so sweet. He accompanied me on guitar. I was shaking so much I was like a phone on vibrate. I was so nervous when I played that. But I really felt something, and I thought oh, this is really fun.

Then my family moved again, and I ended up applying to [public arts high school in a big city]. I wouldn't put it next to the youth orchestra or anything like that.[1] You could tell that the budget for the school was definitely not there. The band room was in the back of the back of the school, far away from everyone else. If we played loud, the band room ceiling tiles would fall down. It was dilapidated. There were roaches and mice, the whole nine yards. But you know, I loved it all.

And if you can believe it, the first [primary instrument] that I ever owned was red, it was literally painted, right, that was the color of the instrument, and I thought it was cool. And that was fine with me. I didn't know about brands or anything like that. I just thought, this looks cool, so I'm going to play that.

We actually ended up coming to visit [undergraduate school] when I was in high school. But we came to see the jazz band because honestly, I didn't even know the school had a classical side. I only ever heard about the jazz band because that was what we talked about at my school.

But initially, I was going to go into medicine. I was trying to be a really good student. I had a lot of academics and extracurriculars, not just playing my instrument. But my mom had cancer, and ended up passing away when I was 15. So I had a crisis, like, oh, my God – do I really want to [be a doctor and] cut into people all day? That doesn't even sound like the kind of thing I want to do.

So, [local university] had a band camp, and I went. At our school that was the one thing that we would get to do in the summer. I spent a lot of time taking care of my family, but that was the one week I could just play [primary instrument]. And the teacher was so cool, just real chill. He said: if you want to do music, you should just do music. And I was like, right, but I want to make money though; I'm not trying to just be broke. But he said, if you try hard enough, it's possible. And I thought, okay, I guess.

He got me in contact with his wife, who was the [primary instrument] teacher at [major conservatory]. But I couldn't afford lessons. At this point, I had one parent and many siblings. So there's no way that I could afford $100 a week to play [primary instrument]. So, oh well, too bad, so sad.

There was this program at [local community music school], where you could audition and get [subsidized] lessons. But the maximum scholarship you could get was 25% of the cost of the lesson. And so I was like, y'all gonna be at 75%? If I have to pay 75%, you might as well say all of it. I literally don't have it.[2]

If it wasn't for the people I know, I would have never made it here. Because after school I would do drumline and jazz band and musicals and I just was always doing something musical. We would actually get gigs. At this point, when I started getting gigs that actually paid money, my dad was like, okay, hold on, this might be something. For Christmas, he got me a [primary instrument], maybe $1,000 bucks, which is a lot of money to me. But I was so happy. That was my baby, I absolutely loved her. I used to just play it literally all the time. Me and my sister shared a room – she can attest, she was tired of it.

So, around October of my senior year I started taking [instrumental] lessons, which is maybe not how people tend to go into classical conservatory life! I learned the exposition of [a major concerto] and [scales] and I thought, this is it, I got all I need. I applied to schools with [medical programs]. And then I applied to [undergraduate institution] and I was like, if I happen to get in, then I'll go, but if not, then whatever, it wasn't meant to be.

When I told my [primary instrument] teacher that I was thinking of applying to [undergraduate institution] first she roasted me. She said, I don't know if you should apply there because they look for talent. I'm like, damn.

Q: Wow.
A: But you know, whatever. Okay, so now I'm just not going to tell her as I continue forward with the audition process.

So, I applied. My counselor told me how to do it but [the application was not received]. I got to my audition and they didn't know who I was. My dad dropped me off. It was so cold outside, and then my dad left, my ride is gone. So, I'm going to have to play something for somebody at this point, like, I don't know what to tell you, I'm not leaving until somebody hears me.

So, [primary teacher] penciled me in at the end of the audition. I'm just getting lost, wandering around the practice rooms for a minute. And I'm hearing people really, like, going in on their instruments! These people know what they are doing.

So, when I went to audition, [the teacher] said "you play better than the instrument you have." And I said, "I can't do anything about that." I mean, it's good to know, but I can't do anything with that information. And she said, "well maybe if you decide to come here, we can work on getting a new instrument." So, okay.

While I was sitting waiting for my dad to come back and pick me up, an administrator came up and said, so we literally don't have an application from you. We have to open up the application, and you have to do it today or tomorrow.

Q: And you were accepted. Wow!

Could you talk about your experiences while you were enrolled [in your bachelor's program], in your classes, with your teacher, and socially?

A: I don't think I relaxed at any point in my time there. I think I was on the whole time. I mean, just to be there, I was working a lot. I don't think I ever really sat back and took a breath, because I was just so afraid of falling behind everyone else. I came to a sample studio class and the stuff that people were playing, it was like, I didn't even know that we could make those sounds, it was like really throwing me. So I'm like, oh my God, I need to **practice** practice.

I was most decidedly rock bottom of my class. I knew it when I came in. But I used to practice like crazy. I hate getting up in the morning. I'm so much more of a night owl than a morning person. But I used to get up at 7 every day to start practicing at 7:30 [am] because I was so scared of just being terrible. And you can only practice so much before you just fall apart.

The second semester of my freshman year was when I actually got to be in the orchestra, and I was terrified within minutes, thinking [the conductor] was going to call me out. You know, my band teacher back home – we have a very familial relationship. He could literally say "What are you doing over there? That was a mess." And it doesn't feel so cold. It feels like we really know each other. So, if he was to say something about whatever I'm doing it, I know how he means it. It doesn't feel like it's like an insult to my ability as an [instrumental] player.

I was really scared of [the conductor]. This guy on the podium, he was so far away! I think my entire first year I was afraid. That would be the best way to describe it. So, I would be in the practice room like a drill sergeant. I'm in there telling myself, you really need these exercises, etudes, everything. I'm playing for hours and hours, and if I'm tired I get a black coffee. I don't like coffee, but it's only because I need the energy. I used to leave [the practice space] at midnight.

I will say, honestly, the academic courses were kind of easy for me. I mean, music theory was hard, but I'm used to working hard in an academic course. So I know how to tackle that. I didn't really know how to do things on [my instrument].

In my first-year studio, there were three international students, me, and then five white people. They were just so gung-ho about it. They would gush and say "oh, my God, did you hear [instrumental professor's] recital the other day?" I used to be so confused. Like, how do we feel it, does it [music] connect to you all the time? Because it's literally just some person [playing their instrument]. It's not the Second Coming. There's no need to do it all like that.[3]

I ended up identifying with students of color more in my second year. I honestly found it to be really strange, because most of those folks are STEM majors, you know what I mean? That's very much like the vibe of wanting to make money and be financially secure for your family. And I want to do that, but I also want to **like** the thing I do. So, it's alienating in a way.

And classical music is such a weird environment. You go to a concert, you can't clap at these times, you can't be too loud, if you're cheering then you're the only one that's loud, and that's like, oh, no. It's just a strange thing. So, it can often be hard to get somebody to come to this hour-and-a-half long orchestra concert.

Q: You mentioned that your studio was mostly white. What else was different from your experience in [high school]?

A: I think...when a white person goes into a space that is all Black, that might be jarring for them. But because of media and whatnot, Black people already know our social standing. So, I knew what I was getting into.

A lot of times, I didn't know all of the music jargon, the vocabulary needed to speak up in the classes. Maybe I know the answer, but I just don't have the words I don't have, so I didn't feel like it was worth talking a lot of the time. It wasn't until maybe my third year that I was, like, honestly, at this point, I couldn't care less what y'all think about me. By the time it felt like an act of revolution, just to speak the way that I would speak normally. I would come in and be like, that piece is boss, I mean, what you want me to say, it slaps and that's how it goes. And they're like, oh, okay.

The elitism is just unreasonable. It was definitely hard to feel like I could say and do things in class. People constantly would say to me, oh, you study jazz? It also really bothered me that in the studio space, when we would have guest artists, I'm the only person who they're like, oh, you're in the studio, too? And I'm like, yeah, I'm here too. Everybody else gets to just be here; why do I have to be questioned? There was also this group of folks who came to sell [primary instrument]. And I promise you, the exact moment that I walked in, the lady said, oh, and we have payment plans. I was like, ok, I don't even want anything y'all have. So that was a lot.

Q: You've mentioned some really challenging experiences that would be very discouraging to or even insurmountable for many people. I'm curious what you felt it was in yourself that allowed you to keep on moving forward and be successful.

A: I feel that. But also, it doesn't feel like that. When people say that, it makes it sound like I really know what I'm doing. It feels like I'm fighting and clawing my way through, it doesn't feel like this was an inspirational story. It feels like it's me in the practice room hitting the same key on the piano for the millionth time trying to match pitch. But afterwards, I guess, it does end up pretty nice.

I will say, my first concert [at school], I came to see the orchestra. And this old lady – I'm sitting in front of her and I just feel a hand in my hair. I'm like, oh my goodness, the petting zoo is closed. Not even so much as a "hey, my name is…" You know what I mean? She just touched me. And she was just investigating, but I was like, this is not the time or the place, and honestly, there is no time and there is no place.

And I'm like, "ok, ma'am," because you can't get mad. The whole angry Black woman thing – I feel like I was never really allowed to be angry about something. It felt like whenever I would be ever so slightly angry, people would be like, oh, well, here she goes, getting pissed off. Okay, now I'm mad because you're saying this, not because of the initial thing! This is the part that's making me angry!

Q: Last question: imagine that you have been invited to have a conversation with the president of a leading American conservatory, and you can give them one piece of advice to improve the environment for Black students. What is that piece of advice?

A: The first thing that comes to mind is vulnerability. I think showing that you're, that we're all people, is important.

For Black students, we already have to work so hard to get just to where we are. If everyone around us seems like they're perfect, then you feel like you're the one flaw in the diamond. If everyone could just be a little more real and just take down the mask, and show that they also make a lot of mistakes, and we also had to do things to get here; and also we've had some instances of privilege, where it was easier for you to get something than it may be for me.

If people were real about how things work, I think that that would help. Honestly, it would help all students, but especially Black students and those who are not from the [standard conservatory] background.

> *It felt like I couldn't be myself in that space and that was when I sort of started creating a shield against people who didn't look like me.*

Latina, Vocal Student, Recent Graduate

This interviewee's gender, racial, and ethnic identities – as a Latina born and raised in Puerto Rico – were very important to her. She is a vocalist who had recently graduated with a Bachelor of Music degree and was pursuing a master of music degree at the time of this interview.

Q: Could you talk about your personal and musical background?
A: I would say that I was born into a musical lineage, a musical family. Both my great grandma and grandma are singers. I wouldn't classify them as classical singers, but their styles were informed by classical technique. They learned to sing from [being involved in] choral music, which is very big in Puerto Rico.

Music has always been part of our community and what links us together in various social settings as well as interpersonal relationships, that's always been something core to our culture and our values. So, they just sang all the time, and I would be listening to them sing with their – I would call them funny vibratos. I would imitate them, and that's how I started to sing.

Every time I visited my grandma, I always wanted to sing with her, and my grandpa would play opera videos. He really wanted me to see what they were doing and just listen and learn as much as I could from videos.

So, I would sit with him in the back of the house, with a small TV, and just listen to [Luciano] Pavarotti. I remember, that was who he would always play. He's like, "See, that's all you have to do." And I was like, "Yeah, sure, for sure, that will happen someday." My early education in voice, it was just all from listening to my family. Also, I joined the choir in church.

I really started singing in the church – it was a very good musical experience, because they teach you devotion. That's something that doesn't come easily, expression and that passion that you learn in the church, you can always bring into your music, and that's something that really, really separates an artist from a singer, just learning how to be expressive. And that's something that you can't learn in a conservatory.

You can take acting classes, but this is something that's just within you naturally, that's something that always sets people of color – and I don't want to generalize, but [referring to] people of color who have similar backgrounds, you know, we learned in church, gospel music for example – that's something that me and my friends [of color] all identified with. I can say that confidently.

Starting in kindergarten, I joined a private school. That was a very big sacrifice for my parents because they come from very, very low-income families. And they just wanted me to be the first person to attend college [from my family]. They said, "You need to learn English. And if you don't learn English, you'll never get a job because those are the people who have the money."

So, I attended this white private Baptist school. It was very religious, and they were very, very devoted – these American missionaries who came to Puerto Rico and really impressed American culture onto the school.

They wouldn't allow us to speak Spanish in the hallway. They wanted us to look a certain way – we couldn't wear earrings. It felt like I couldn't be myself in that space and that was when I sort of started creating a shield against people who didn't look like me. Because they were so strict! We weren't allowed to dance. I remember one time I wore a skirt that was in the middle of my knees, not below my knees, and they kept me in a room praying until my mom picked me up. That kind of feeling, as a nine-year old, really traumatized me. And I thought all white Americans were that way, you know?

But musically, it was a good experience for me, because I met [an important teacher] who led my first structured musical experience. We started preparing for our first vocal competition, and this choral director from [major music school in the area] came to work with us. She was this Afro-Puerto Rican woman who did not look like any student or teacher at our school. And I just remember just loving her. She just came in with such a vibrant positive energy, laughing very loud and was just not at all like the other teachers that I had there. They were missing the element of passion – they have such strict norms of how they had to act in front of the students, that they weren't allowed to just be themselves, you know.

This teacher, she just came in laughing and talking to us, saying "Why are you guys so serious, you have to smile, why are you guys like this?" You know, we were so [emotionally] deprived. Musically, you have to be able to just be yourself and be genuine with the music. She brought that into the choir. She's an amazing director. I've never had such a passionate director, and she's so good with everything that she does, musically, vocally.

I remember one of her last workshops with us. She just pointed at me, she was like, "You, come into the back with me." Like, "Oh, God, what's going on?," I thought.

So, we went to the back of the room. It was this prayer room, the same prayer room where I was held for wearing that skirt. She asked me, "Do you really like singing?" And I said, "Yes, I do!" She said, "I want to give you a free voice lesson. Come to my house. You are going to be my student." My mom was there, and my mom was like, yes, yes, yes, yes to everything. My mom is very dedicated.

So, I took my first lesson with her. And she said to me "You are going to be big. You have so much potential. I haven't heard a voice like yours in years, and I need to work with you." Nobody had ever said those words to me before. My mom couldn't really afford lessons. And it cost 30 bucks a lesson. That was a lot for my mom. I remember the teacher said, "Don't worry, don't pay me for this lesson." And she was also low income, my teacher, you know, so it was a lot for her to say, "Don't pay me," because she needed the money as well.

She was training me musically in everything – aural skills, note reading. "This is a major scale, that is a minor scale." And she started giving me all the tools so that I could enter the music [preparatory] school. [The teachers there] are very tough. The same teachers that teach there [are] in the conservatory. All the great musicians from Puerto Rico, I would say 60% of all the great names have gone through that school. Bomba, Latin jazz, classical, you name it – they prepare you in such a way that you are able to express yourself musically in any genre. She trained me and she gave me a couple of art songs. I learned them by heart. And I got into the school.

My first day in this school, people were so confident. All of the instruction was in Spanish. I took music appreciation, which was like [introductory music history in college]. But they teach the music of our Puerto Rican ancestors and our genres. And they do not start with this medieval music – they say that music started with percussion and voice, which is probably true. I mean, when people first created music, it would be with our bodies, basically. And then we created instruments to be able to do all of these other things, but we are music, we are the ones who say what is music and what is not. So, it started with us, I think.

Q: Once you arrived at [undergraduate institution] for college, what were some of the cultural differences that you noticed?

A: All the cultural differences – they were very hard for me. I cried so much. And my parents saw me cry and felt guilty, but at the same time they were doing something that really allowed me to attend [college].

Here's one example of the differences. When I meet someone, I remember them. We met, and I'm going to assume the best of you. You know, I'm going to consider you my friend because we're in a community. Everybody in your school, that's your community and there shouldn't be negativity or competition, we're here to help each other.

But I remember just meeting people [in school], and then those people would pass me by the hallway not looking at me and not making eye contact. It just takes a very long time to really make friends and approach people because people are not approachable. They're taught to be individualistic, and to just focus on their successes. I feel like culturally, in the Caribbean, you're taught to work with people and alone, you can't…when I rise, you rise, because we're a community. [In that context, even if there] is gossip and everybody knows your business, it's because they care. [In college] I wanted people to be in on my business, I wanted to have friends who were really invested in me and I wanted to really be invested in my friends. And that's why I got hurt by people, because I'm very invested in people, you know. That was something that was very hard for me, and I felt very alone. Without community, without people, I did not feel myself. In the United States, it was just, like, I felt alone. And that was very hard for me.[4]

Q: In college, how else did you experience feeling isolated, or alienated, or culturally misunderstood?

A: I remember teachers telling me "I don't think you really prepared for this." That was very hard for me to hear that because I have always been so prepared for everything, you know, I had been a shining star.

Q: Did that feel accurate, when they said they didn't perceive that you were prepared?

A: I think, you know, for some things I wasn't prepared at the moment. But that's what college is about. I can get prepared because I have the skill sets. You know, I have the work ethic, and I have the eagerness, and I'm a very eager person and I was able to overcome that within the first year, within the first semester.

I just needed somebody to take me under their wing and explain things.[5] I mean, nobody ever taught me how to go to college, nobody taught me how to write a formal paper in the American style, or how to use MLA or Chicago style or anything like that. I just needed people to teach me that, even just very briefly. And I would get it easily. I mean, we come from families that have struggled, we have learned to overcome so many traumas and to follow our dreams. We are very eager people, and people who want to learn and grow. So, I could do it, and I knew I could do it.

Q: In college, did you have a general perception that your identity was relevant in terms of how you were treated or how you navigated situations, especially vocally?

A: Well, yes. This is a very big debate in the world of vocal technique and pedagogy.

So, there's a lot of debate in voice [as to whether] blind auditions are necessary because there is this theory that people of color have bigger voices, or we have darker voices. Yeah, there's a big debate. It's wrong, you know?

Q: There's actually a book about that specifically, called The Race of Sound.

A: Yes, I know it. That's right. Also, I remember in a certain opera role, for the character I was playing, people were like, "you need to move your hips. You know how to move your hips, right? Just move your hips! Just do it."

And I was like, oh, I feel uncomfortable. I'm not moving my hips for you. Yes, I can move my hips – what are you

really asking me to do when you're saying that, though? You know, why tell me to do that in front of everybody? Right? That's just like, not cool. And in the middle of rehearsal?
I was challenged with things like that all the time, requests to "bring your passion," "bring your Spanish," "bring your flair."

At a point, I decided, you know what, I'm just going to isolate myself because I felt that people were fake. [Other students] would act friendly but were not invested in the same way that I was ready to be invested in a new relationship, and care deeply. So, I was like, I'm not wasting my energy on people who do not understand the degree of care that is necessary to be part of a community. So, that really turned me off. I isolated myself from the department.

Q: So, that's not uncommon. I've talked to voice students at a range of schools who identify as Black or Latinx and who felt the need, at some point, to isolate themselves away from their voice department, for various reasons that they usually identify as cultural.

It's a little funny because, I mean, voice students feeling that other voice students are being fake – that's not exactly a novel complaint, right? But what you're suggesting is that the way in which that's practiced in conservatories in the United States by a mostly white student body is culturally specific as well. It is going to be different from ways in which voice students from other backgrounds might feel that they should be interacting.

This emphasis on community v. individual orientation always comes up when comparing white American culture to almost any other culture – American culture is the most individualistic and competitive – and we consider that to be a normal frame of reference when it's really not. It's culturally situated. All of that takes on a different valence in a conservatory environment where competition is already heightened, and interactions are fraught.

A: Yes. There were a lot of backhanded comments. And I received questions like "Where are you from? How do you learn there?" "Are there McDonalds in Puerto Rico?" I remember that question. Or like, "Oh, you're an international student? Do you need me to read slower to you?"

I mean, some things did take me a little longer because I did actually learn them in another language first, you know, but still.

I just had a lot of questions that I wish I could have asked somebody genuinely without being looked at weirdly. Without community, it's very hard to feel comfortable asking those questions. Because you feel like you are putting yourself down when you're already down. You know, you're putting yourself lower, you're really putting yourself in a hole. So, it's very hard.

Q: What do you think is necessary to drive further curricular inclusion, particularly in the area of voice? How should we go about those efforts?

A: You know, it's very hard. It's a very hard question. Because with students comes music. I was arguing that there should be more Latin music in the conservatory. Yes, there should. But that's the same thing a student from Hong Kong is going to say [about their music], it's the same thing a person from India is going to say. With students comes music. It's very hard to diversify it in a way that it represents everybody.

I think it's a matter of not putting white music on a pedestal and explaining that these elements were not the only thing going on in history. And also, we [students of color] decided to go in the classical direction because that's what we liked; but also, yes, there are people of color making music. Not just looking at [Ludwig van] Beethoven and [Johann Sebastian] Bach and [Wolfgang Amadeus] Mozart, but really digging into what are women composers doing, what are female composers doing? What does sonata form really mean?

We talk about how beautiful this music is. Yes, it is beautiful. Yes, it sounds good to the ears. But let's talk about colonization, let's talk about the arabesque and orientalism, all of that stuff. Let's really unpack these things and really know what we're doing, so that we can inform our performances and inform how we talk about music.

Q: What are your thoughts on diversifying opera specifically?

A: Opera is a beautiful genre, and it's also a white form, a white genre. It came from [Claudio] Monteverdi, recitatives, oratorios, this is all influenced by the church, you know – the settings of opera. I'm not saying [similar musical practices] didn't happen in other communities, but the specific way we chose to do this comes from that background. I think there are operas that are very, very racist that should not be performed. There's others that could [be rehabilitated] if we breathe new life into them by working on character development, reflecting on how the narrative connects with us today. And we need more composers of color, more young composers – there are operas today that are cool, you know?

Q: Casting is a huge issue in opera as well, because many roles are historically limited to a specific voice type and physical appearance. Can we move past that?

A: I think that nobody should have to look a certain way. You know, if we're casting for a princess, anybody can be a princess. I mean, anybody can be a mother or father. And if there's a couple, usually the man is taller, the woman's shorter. But what if your Susanna is tall? What if your Susanna is Black? I mean, you know – what's the problem?

Q: What would you say to younger students of color who are entering musical training programs right now?

A: My first piece of advice is to know who you are. Every time I go into a stage, I am myself. I bring my identity into every piece of music that I perform. And the first thing that I tell everybody that I meet is "I'm from Puerto Rico. Who are you, and where are you from?"

My second piece of advice is to have open conversations with everyone. Understand that a lot of the generations that are working in music right now are old school. Trying to have conversations without judgment in your heart – there's always going to be judgment for both parties – but letting that die down and having conversations where both parties can grow is very important. Don't get offended. I mean, of course, you will get offended. But before you need to burst into tears, try to listen – because there's always some sort of truth in everything that people have to say, even if it's twisted.

At the same time, try to bring your own perspective to the table in a way that they can listen to it. Not just that you're giving them all of this information, all of your feelings, and all of your criticism because they're not being inclusive. Bring them in and be like, hey, let's have a conversation. I want you to listen to what I'm feeling, I want you to listen to where I come from, I want you to understand what made me feel this way, and I want you to understand why we should keep moving forward together. How can we make this work? How can we combine forces? Who else can partner with us on this? I feel like just having those kinds of conversations is important. Maybe it's just me, because I love to talk and I love to connect with everybody.

What I would tell students of color and students with various identities and from various communities is – just say what you want to do and what you need. If you say it, eventually somebody's going to listen to you and you're going to see change.

A lot of organizations also want to get away from this elitist notion that the orchestra is for the top 1% of our societies, and a good way to do that is just to not be that. Don't program music that only the 1% is interested in.

African-American, Orchestral Player, Mid-career

This interviewee identified as a cisgender African-American male. He had earned B.M. and M.M. degrees in instrumental performance more than a decade before the interview. At the time of the interview, he held a tenured symphony orchestra position and was a professor at local state university.

Q: Can you talk a little bit about your personal and musical background prior to attending a conservatory?
A: My mom is an elementary school music teacher in the public schools. So, I actually started [instrument other than primary instrument] when I was three years old. My mom was my first instrumental teacher, although I don't really remember any of that. My first [primary instrument] teacher was, no pun intended, pretty instrumental in my development as a person and as an [instrumentalist] and really had an enormous impact on my life. She was like a second mom to me, extremely intellectual, a great teacher. I got really lucky at every stage to be surrounded by people like that, and to have

Interviews with Young Professionals 95

parents who really thought classical music was important. They invested a lot of time and money into activities for us, even besides classical music.

My dad was also a trumpet player and a classical music fan. My extended family was really into jazz and ragtime. Music was just in our house all the time, and part of our culture growing up. Besides that, I had a really supportive close relationship with my music teachers. I had a private teacher and I was part of a youth orchestra when I was in high school.

Growing up in [city of origin], it was also pretty diverse. I was probably one of two Black people, of course [playing classical music]. …But I was never made to feel like an outsider, because there was such a large Black population – culturally [that city] has a lot of Black culture that just kind of pervades everything so that it was as easy as it could have been. The only time I ever had to deal with racial or other types of bullying was in high school.

Q: You had a number of other teachers who were really seminal in your development prior to college, right? Were those teachers all throughout elementary and high school? Were they mostly white?

A: They were all white, except for my mom, of course. But the main teacher that I had for most of my life was a white South African woman who actually expatriated because she hated Apartheid. Expatriated isn't even the right word. She was not given permission by the government to leave her country. So she lived in exile for decades before she could get her American citizenship. She wasn't allowed to go back to South Africa, and I'm not really sure she ever did. I studied with her until I was 18.

She was highly educated, very socially aware, spoke multiple languages, was an avid reader of books. A collector of knowledge. The rare times I would hear her talk about South Africa, it was about her family, or things that she missed. And you could tell how sorry she was that things were the way they were in South Africa, and how the only thing she felt she could do was to escape, to move where that wasn't happening – or, happening to a lesser degree.

I would stay at her house for weeks at a time. We took a trip to Sweden together for a [instrument] festival. I was kind of like her assistant and would have lessons more frequently than just once a week. I think it kind of set me up well for my relationship with my college teacher. [In college,] it was the same kind of nurturing of my development.

Q: It sounds like you don't have many specific recollections of incidents that felt racist, for the majority of your education prior to college.

A: Yeah, [my parents were] really, very supportive and tried to shield us from all that. They made sure we were having experiences where we could just exist without really having to be exposed to any sort of prejudice or racism. If I did experience anything like that, it was never explicit racism.

Q: Recently, conservatories have begun an effort to "diversify the curriculum." I'm curious what your view is of curricular diversity when you were a student.

A: The education I had was strictly Western and European. There was never any mention of Black composers, even their influence on people like [Antonín] Dvořák. I learned most of what I know about Black composers or non-classical Black genres of music only outside of school or well after graduating. I had never heard of Florence Price or was aware that Duke Ellington wrote classical music. I never heard [music by] George Walker played at recitals in school.

Part of the issue is that there are not a lot of Black professors or Black students in conservatories. But also, you play what your teacher tells you to play. Even Black students – we're just playing the same music. There are a lot of [Johannes] Brahms sonatas getting thrown around, and other standard repertoire.

For instance, in graduate school, I took a semester-long class on J.S. Bach. It was an incredible in-depth class about a composer I really care about. There is just nothing else even approaching that [for Black composers]. In many high schools, you might encounter an African-American Studies class; there was no equivalent to that in [conservatory].[6]

Q: Do you remember any social interactions in school that had racialized elements?

A: I remember there was a guitarist from Mississippi who was always being racially provocative. He had never really talked to a lot of Black people. He was just curious to know "what the deal was." To be around him and hear these sorts of questions was always a little weird, because I never had to think about that. Nothing ever like that before. ...questions like, "Do Black people all eat this? What do you think of this racially charged joke?" Or like, "What's the deal with the N-word?" Now, that is a lot right there, you know?

But in [undergraduate program and graduate school] I had a relatively diverse and very, very supportive group of friends. When I talked to [my undergraduate studio teacher] recently, I thanked him for shielding us in his studio from bad behavior and attitudes that may have been going on outside the studio.

A: It's really important to have a teacher like that.

Q: Yeah. And that's, I think, been the constant in each of the phases of my life, just having a couple of key people that had enough power to protect their students, to protect me, from whatever nonsense existed out there.

But I feel like Black people growing up in classical music is already not, like, a normal sampling of the culture.

Q: Could you expand on that, on what you mean by that exactly?

A: It's a lot of work to get a kid into classical music. It takes really dedicated parents with the financial means to get an instrument, to get lessons, and time to take you to those events. And the socioeconomic status of African-Americans [is not always excellent].

So those with those resources have a very different life. Some Black professional classical musicians come from middle-class, college-educated households. That is not the norm.[7] Both of my parents were into music and there was classical music in the house. I mean, I could identify Bach. One of my first words was "Pachelbel" when I was super little. Jazz and ragtime, I was pretty familiar with that. There was a piano in our house and me and my brothers all played.

That was just unusual compared to the standard American household. And so when you get to that conservatory level, you're already dealing with people who have spent most of their lives doing this stuff. It's unusual. I think it's similar for high-level athletes. To ask [African-American conservatory students] about the average Black experience is not always going to give you a very representative answer, based on [their upbringing].

Q: Do you feel that you had musically diverse educational experiences, the kind that would be necessary to prepare students to be effective practitioners as teachers and players in the modern world? Do you feel that your education generally prepared you for work as a professional?

A: So, let me answer that last question first. Absolutely not, and on no level other than the orchestra audition.

I've heard this from other musicians my parents' age, I'm hearing this from musicians that are my students' age: once you win a competition or a job – this is especially true for orchestra auditions – now, you have this job, and now you've got to show up, but no one prepares you for the fact that now you've got a different program every week. Or every week, you've got a different concerto in a new city. There were many holes in my music education. It would have been nice to have some education about what's expected of professionals, and the inner workings of how ensembles function. You know, how do you run a chamber group? How do you build a website, what do you do in an orchestra committee, what do you do in an orchestra beyond just being prepared to play the rep? And there wasn't anything in our education that prepared me for any of that.

Having played in [a major metropolitan area] and having been exposed to musical diversity there makes it a lot easier for me to play pop concerts. I don't feel like a complete square when we're doing something with a jazz group, or I don't have to turn down a gig when I'm asked to write something for a gospel choir. That really isn't a ton of money, but that has put a couple extra bucks in my pocket, just knowing what to do with that music.

Q: Playing in some groups melding classical, hip-hop, and jazz, groups that were labeled "crossover," I recall thinking that this is what popular classical music – a classical music that is **popular** – should look and sound like. But that style is denigrated in many circles and lacks mainstream acceptance. What can we do to combat that, or is that something we need to combat?

A: Yeah, I don't quite understand why that is because all orchestras are 501c3 nonprofit organizations. [To diversify programming] seems obvious, and it really creates the opportunity to do something special for your community. Each city has its own diverse community. Orchestras are talking more and more about how to cater specifically to our resident communities. So that's the first thing, I think you've got an opportunity to get more dollars in the door, more butts in the seats.

A lot of organizations also want to get away from this elitist notion that the orchestra is for the top 1% of our societies, and a good way to do that is just to not be that. Don't program music that only the 1% is interested in. Try to at least meet your audience halfway, so that people feel comfortable and feel like the orchestra is for them, that it's not something just for "those" sorts of people, but that it's a city institution, just in the same way a sports team is. I think that creates a lot more economic opportunity for the institution. And it is a bit of a mystery to me why leadership ever resists this. I think it's just inertia. It's hard for people to change. But now's a good time to start.

For the orchestras not doing that, it's going to be harder and harder to justify your status as a nonprofit organization if you're just appealing to the elites. Orchestras are mostly surviving through tax dollars, donations, and the goodwill of local citizens. At some point, if politicians or citizens don't feel like it's worth their time or money, then it really puts you in a really tough spot in terms of your survival, and also, of course, it challenges the survival of classical music.

Q: Can you say more about the necessity of diversity in performance training?

A: I think being as flexible as an artist is going to be more and more important as we kind of move forward into the future. Unfortunately, [in school] I didn't even play any Brahms symphonies, I don't think I had played all of Beethoven's symphonies. If you can't play the standards, I think that's going to be a bigger problem as things get more competitive.

But I also think, if you've never heard gospel, if you've never been exposed to jazz, and, you know, someone asked you to do something like that in an orchestra, and you've got a week of rehearsals or less to get it done, and you just can't hack it, I think that it's going to be really, really, really difficult for you to be successful professionally, especially as more advanced techniques like improvisation, for instance, come in to your space and people require musicians who can do that sort of things.

I think you're already starting to see this with aspects of chamber music, where it's not just enough to show up to a gig and play. You have to be good at differentiating what you do from what everybody else in a quartet does, which includes web design and getting your message across.

It's not just a matter of diversifying for diversification's sake; it's a matter of diversifying for financial survival, to stay relevant in your community and relevant to the larger art form at large. Most orchestras are not going to be able to do 50 "classics" programs a year. It's going to take diverse programming.

What could help orchestras is to have more people on staff, more people on the board, more of the decision makers in the room, from diverse backgrounds, to make sure that these things are not just being accomplished but are accomplished in a sensitive and sensible way. I've seen a number of organizations making a lot of mistakes, trying to do the best they can on some of this stuff, and some not doing the best they can. So yeah, these sorts of things, I think are going to become more and more important. And I think that the area of control for organizations is hiring on the staff level and on the board level.

Q: So, you know, it's funny, because something naturally that I observed myself, that we've been working in this way toward diversifying classical music, towards diversifying orchestras for several decades. But the numbers are not yet radically changing. Do you have any insight into why that is?

A: There just aren't enough educational programs pursuing [students of color]. I mean, in [my hometown], the Suzuki program had thousands of kids from the area. Most of them were not from the inner city, most of them were not African American, there was just no outreach to that community. In my Black community, there wasn't a whole lot of understanding of why [Suzuki training] was important. And so, we're kind of between a rock and a hard place. You have to help parents understand that it's important, that's something worth pursuing. I think a lot of you don't know what your kid is going to be good at until you expose them to it. But I think a lot of potentially really great Black classical musicians are just never exposed to it.

And then there are the ones who might not have the financial means to pursue it. That's something I encounter all the time in teaching. A lot of kids are super passionate about it, but their parents aren't willing to spend the time or the money for them to pursue it, because they just don't think it's important, they think their kids need to be doing something to make money, and I totally understand that.

This is a financially risky career. The overhead is extremely high, lessons are expensive, instruments are extremely expensive. The chance of establishing a financially successful career is extremely low. In the long run, a lot of American culture is focused on – what can we do right now that's going to get us paid? I run up against those ideas [from parents and students], like, why is this important? This isn't immediately useful, how am I going to use this later? And so, I can understand those sorts of barriers, you know, before you're even signing up for your first lesson, you know, those are things that I think are fairly apparent to parents.

But to help people get over that obstacle, the first thing we have to do is to help parents understand that this is important because it's culturally fulfilling, and it's also going to make you very good at other things.

And, we have to help orchestras understand that it's important to invest in the nine-year old. [Some orchestral players] say that they only take advanced students. My question is, well, where do they come from? If it's not from us, no one else is here to do this work.

Q: This book questions the extent to which some students of color feel assimilated into conservatory environments – culturally, aesthetically, in terms of speech, dress, personal behavior, all those kinds of things. I was curious to what extent that resonates with you.

A: So, I mean, how I was brought up and where I grew up – mostly in the suburbs, around the sorts of people who are playing classical music – I feel that culturally, my family, my uncles, and aunts, and cousins, we're all kind of already there, in terms of mainstream white American culture. We're going to college, we have professional, white-collar jobs.

In any professional area, there's going to be a certain amount of assimilation. For instance, you're going to have to dress a certain way. I cannot wear whatever I want to a concert; there's a very specific dress code. If you're working in an office, there's a professional dress code. The problem becomes, then, you know, if you are abiding by that dress code and have a hairstyle that is not allowed by rule, or that that your boss doesn't, like – in our case, in rehearsal, if there's something that you're wearing that is found objectionable, by someone else, especially peer-to-peer, then yeah, those things can become problematic really, really fast.

And unfortunately, this was the only part of my career, only part of my life, where I've really experienced just outward, clumsy racism, professionally, mostly from conductors or audience members. When I found myself dealing with problems, I took them to HR. And I found out very quickly that HR is there to protect the institution, not necessarily the individual worker. It will ultimately be up to staff or the board to decide what happens, and a lot of times they're not going to want to rock the boat. And even the union is here to protect your job, so if one union member appears to attack another union member, they are going to go after the person [they believe] is the attacker, not stand up for the victim. That was super disheartening to discover fairly early on. So, there's that sort of problem – it's not even just assimilation, it's just straight-up injustice. You know, the powerful are there to protect each other.

This is one of those areas where I don't think musicians are adequately prepared in school – about how work rules function in places of business. Especially for Black musicians, who are carrying a distinct, and I think, very valuable culture into these institutions – the institutions are not prepared to handle them. If there's no work rule that says you can't wear a dashiki and dreads at work, you should be able to do that. And unfortunately, we often find out that a person in power will object to it. And then that becomes the new rule, but it's not contractually obligated or written down anywhere, and still because you're the subordinate you need to abide by this rule.

That would be my number one piece of advice: If you can put yourself in a position to have more authority in your institutions, do it. If you can join the board of the orchestra, if you can join the orchestra committee, you can make decisions about how things are carried out.

Or even better yet, join your local union. I attended a union convention a number of years ago, and it was almost exclusively white men over 50. I think this was in a big convention space in Las Vegas. There must have been 1,000 people in that room, and I counted maybe four Black people, and maybe a dozen women, and maybe another 20 or 30 people under the age of 50. So, you can imagine how if you're a certain age, race, and gender, and in charge, maybe you're not going to be the most up-to-date on best practices, or how race relations have changed in the past several decades.

So that's it. You have to assimilate to a certain extent in any workplace, and unfortunately, that's kind of always how it is. In order to change, it's going to be necessary for Black people to assert that a lot of American culture is Black culture, that we exist, and that it's not the Reagan era anymore. We can't just be ignored anymore, even if only for economic reasons.

Q: To finish up – imagine you are having a conversation with the president of a major orchestra. And you can only give them one piece of advice to improve the conditions for musicians in the orchestra, and to improve the audience's experience. What is that one piece of advice?

A: Get help. You can hire consultants to diversify your programming. There are people who specialize in this area, and whose whole job it is to come in, take a look at your city, do interviews with your orchestra, the number of people on your board, your staff, the community, and then to recommend how you should go about things in the most efficient way so that you're not reinventing the wheel.

And that's the big problem. I think a lot of organizations don't have the time, or the money, or the energy, or even the will to do this sort of research, but there are people who have already done the work and are willing to come in and make a custom program for you. And it generally doesn't cost very much, compared to the benefit. So that's one thing, try not to reinvent the wheel.

But even if you have the best of intentions, if you don't have staff diversity when developing these programs, then you're probably either going to make a lot of poor choices that don't end up moving the needle, or at worse, a lot of bad choices that end up alienating people. I see a lot of that.

As far as I know, a white man would almost never doubt why he got a job.

African-American, Doctoral Student in an Academic Field, Background in Instrumental Performance

This interviewee identified as cisgender, male, heterosexual, and African-American. He came from a middle-class background and earned an undergraduate degree in instrumental performance, followed by a master's degree in an academic field in music. At the time of the interview, he was completing a doctorate in that field.

Q: Can you talk a little bit about your personal and musical background prior to attending your bachelor's program?

A: I spent my childhood in [Midwestern suburban neighborhood], which is like an upper middle-class neighborhood about 40 minutes outside of [major city]. I had access to good music education, and when I was in fifth grade, I just kind of gravitated towards [primary instrument]. I had private lessons, and I played in a youth orchestra starting in 10th grade.

I think it fit into this larger picture of my parents wanting to make sure that I had a good profile for college. Since I gravitated towards music, that's what I mostly did. I did sports far less, especially in high school.

Q: And was there any kind of music prevalent in your house? Classical music, other kinds of music?

A: There was a lot of jazz being played in the house on the radio. My parents being of the Baptist faith, there was a lot of gospel music, sometimes in the house, sometimes on the radio, but definitely [we were] going to church every Sunday. There wasn't any classical music being played. I remember that – when I started getting into classical music and started playing it on the radio, my family was not thrilled about that. But they did support my playing classical music. And my dad played a bit of piano and organ in church. My mom likes music, but she doesn't sing or play anything. And my brothers were musical too – one played trombone and one played cello. I was the first one to get started [playing] just because I was the oldest.

Q: And was there a particular teacher or an ensemble experience that really nudged you in this direction?

A: The specific choice to start playing [primary instrument] was a bit random. I knew that I liked music. The teacher I had in grade school and high school was an important mentor, because she introduced me to the instrument, and also conducted the high school orchestra, and also she is a Black woman. She was definitely an important figure. Once I started taking private lessons, that was the motivator, having someone like that invested in my personal growth. And also, there was a general spirit of competitiveness in middle school and high school, I think, once I started playing in the Youth Symphony. Seeing other people play really well, that made me want to improve.

Q: Can you talk a bit about your experiences at [your undergraduate institution] in your academic classes, with your music teachers, and socially?

A: The way [that school] works is nice – there's a school of music and it felt like everyone knew everyone in the school, more or less. It was a nice community. In my middle and high school, and also at [college,] there were very few people of color, or at least, very few Black or Latinx people, and it wasn't until my freshman or sophomore year that I started paying more attention and started caring more about that.

Questions of belonging then started to play a role. As my career shows, I had a very strong academic bent, so by the end of my freshman year, I was really into [academic study of a musical area]. Eventually I ended up pivoting, but there was this sense that my [instrumental] performance was not as good as I wanted to be, and it kind of added to this general sense of not belonging, that I think, even if I wasn't fully conscious of it, was racially based.

Even though I came from a socioeconomic background that was equivalent to if not better than a lot of my peers, there was still that feeling of distance, culturally. That all came even more to a head in [graduate school]. Even though my family didn't listen to classical music growing up, there are families that do that, and they just have different cultural contexts. And I felt like I was lacking, for a while, whether it be knowing music repertoire, or feeling comfortable in a museum, talking about art, stuff that – to put it crudely, could be grouped under "white people" stuff – I didn't always feel like I fit in.[8]

And as I got involved in [academic field], I gradually came to feel that I more or less fit into the spaces that I occupy now. But there were some growing pains there, I would say. I do wonder whether my colleagues or teachers [felt] it was a little odd that I was drawn to and was excelling in [my academic field]. In my education experience overall – you know, I was a smart guy taking some AP classes, or other advanced classes, etc. – I just generally was in spaces where not a lot of other Black people would be in those classes. That same phenomenon existed in [graduate school].

Q: And your high school was mostly white?

A: It wasn't the whitest school ever – there were people of different races, ethnicities, and cultures represented – but there were mostly white people there.

Q: Do you feel like the racial composition of your close friend group was pretty much the same or different in high school, your undergrad program, and your grad program? Did you feel like you were in mostly white friend groups, or in more diverse friend groups, or with groups of mostly Black friends?

A: I'd say mostly white, but also other people of color, not anything specific. We're just in the same circle, either because I like them and we're cool, or maybe we've perhaps bonded over some sort of "people of color" thing. I don't know. But I feel like that's been relatively consistent across the board.

I guess the one thing that has always made me feel a little uncomfortable, though – it's just been interesting to me that like in mostly white spaces, I feel pretty at ease, because that's just kind of like what I've been around all my life. But then if I'm in a majority Black space, I can't always feel at ease in those. I often feel myself going, oh, now there are all these other Black people, and I don't talk like most of them, am I being judged on my Blackness? Do I feel comfortable here? It's just interesting how those questions have come up a lot.

In middle and high school, undergrad, and in grad school, I've just always been in spaces where Black people and people of color were not the majority. So my social life has always taken that path.

Q: You're doing such high-level work in majority white spaces and in one of the whiter fields in academia, structurally, ideologically, philosophically, etc. I'm curious as to what extent you believe that your perception, or the perception of others of yourself, as a Black person operating at a high level in a majority-white space, has the potential to impact your performance?

A: I think it definitely has, even though I'm sure it hasn't always been conscious, and when thinking in broader terms – like, do I feel like I belong here – as soon as I question that and give that too much weight, then it does affect me. You know, even back in the day of the appeal of [a] performance [career], I think that was a factor because, you know, if I don't feel like I belong there, then it makes it like when I'm practicing or preparing…can I do this, or is this for me, or is it not? That feeling of imposter syndrome was always present.[9]

I've often [suffered from] imposter syndrome because I had a lot of success getting into grad school. I applied… to five [graduate] programs and got into all five, and I was feeling really great. But then, you know, it slowly started to sink in: Do people want me just because I'm the only Black [student in this area] who they think is good enough, and they're concerned about diversity in their programs? I think that affected my performance starting off [in grad school] because there were a lot of growing pains. I think some were normal for students, like reading more difficult texts, etc., but there was also this question of, "Am I cut out to do this?" Or did they just see my application and then say, "We'll go with him, because it would be good for us'"? So it wasn't until I actually passed qualifying exams that I could tell myself a bit more firmly, "I did it, I'm here, I survived this far, I've got what it takes."

Right now in the job market, it's sort of the same phenomenon. I feel more certain of myself, my identity now. But, [the racial challenges are] even more pointed, because there are people saying that they want to diversify their faculty, making target/opportunity hires. These days, it affects my performance less, because I'm coming to terms with my identity as a Black person who isn't someone's stereotypical idea of a Black person, feeling like, well, this is my identity and who I am, etc.

Q: I'm really glad you mentioned that issue of what's happening right now in terms of the intersection of identity and hiring, because it's really challenging for all of us [people of color] in academia. It would be impossible, I think, to be hired in a way that felt completely free of all that encumbrance, because even if you chose not to identify your race, everyone would know who you are.

So there's little you could do to divorce yourself from a perception of your identity, for better or worse, when you're hired. That's the reality that we have to deal with. I'm curious what your advice or thoughts would be for younger students who might be thinking of going into your field or something similar, but are concerned about how to navigate that or whether the perception of their identity will override everything else they have to offer?

A: Yeah, that's a great question. And it's something I'm still figuring out. One piece of advice that I've gotten is this: As far as I know, a white man would almost never doubt why he got a job. It's not like, "Did I get this because I'm a white man?" You know, that's just not in the culture. So why should I harbor doubts just because I'm a Black person?

The other response that I have is that, you know, it's like this huge Catch-22. Because there are all these times when, even if people don't want to admit it, like your Blackness is – I don't want to say it's like holding us back – but there are all these structural barriers to people who are Black. And then as soon as there's some way that we could benefit, it's like,

"Whoa, whoa, whoa, why are we talking about race here?" And it's like, you know, I've been Black this whole time. It feels like I would need to hide it.

And even when I write personal statements, I'm not saying "I'm Black" in every sentence, but I've gotten a little bit more confident in not being afraid to mention it. You know, who are we kidding ourselves in thinking that this is all fair to begin with.

So, I guess what I would say to a younger scholar or performer, or even a younger version of myself, is – just do your thing. There will always be people who want to say you got where you got because you're Black. You could do all this stuff to try to prove them wrong. And it will never happen. You'll never convince certain people. So just live your life.

Notes

1 Students who do not have access to early training are already limited in their choices for further training by middle school and high school. Even if eligible for a public arts school (potentially underfunded), they may not be competitive for or be able to afford prestigious youth orchestra programs run by major orchestras. In 2021, tuition for the Boston Youth Symphony Orchestra was $1,600 per year, about 5% of the median income of $35,000 in Roxbury, MA – Boston's majority Black and Latinx neighborhood.
2 For low-income students, partial scholarships may be functionally meaningless, and even potentially insulting. To offer financial aid benefits an institution's image, but makes no functional difference if the remaining balance is too large a percentage of household income.
3 It is worth reflecting on the classical music community's encouragement of a culture of "hero worship," excessive valuation and cult-like status assigned to living performers and composers, besides canonical ones. This culture is problematic for many reasons, not the least of which is its facilitation of psychological and sexual abuse.
4 The interviewee uses "United States" to refer to the U.S. mainland, in distinction to the island of Puerto Rico.
5 This interviewee articulates some needs that could be met by a formal staff position dedicated to student support, but additional training for faculty would might also be necessary.
6 While the obvious conservatory equivalent of an "African-American Studies" class would be a course examining works by composers self-identified as African-American, this is not at all a corollary to the

in-depth theoretical work and cultural analysis foregrounded in a typical African-American studies course. Perhaps an ideal version of such a course would be premised on a theoretical and cultural analysis of the origins of African-American classical music.
7 According to the Education Trust, in 2016, about 14% of African-Americans held a four-year Bachelor Degree and 7.8% had earned a graduate degree. https://edtrust.org/wp-content/uploads/2014/09/Black-Degree-Attainment_FINAL.pdf
8 The interviewee refers to a well-known term. The blog "Stuff White People Like" was so popular that it inspired several books.
9 The interviewee's reflection highlights the relationship between imposter syndrome and stereotype threat, in which fear of confirming a negative stereotype leads to underperformance.

Conclusion

It should not be an enormous surprise that many young people of color report that they do not feel welcome or comfortable in majority-white Western classical music spaces. A popular solution has been to boost the volume in the "pipeline" – the cohort of students of color receiving training at a young age. Increasing the number of artists of color is absolutely likely to result in some change. In the past few decades, many of these artists and groups have exhibited incredible aesthetic creativity in the incorporation of improvisation and other aesthetics, but increased demographic diversity alone is not enough to induce targeted and concentrated change in environments with a history of exclusion.

In conservatories, the manner of dress, speech, and so forth expected by teachers on stage and in class conforms to white norms. The production of more artists of color who are fully assimilated into these norms runs directly counter to the goal of genuine diversity in the expression of Western classical music. (We should be dismayed by the prospect that Western classical music participation might become more diverse while its musical content does not.)

Another argument against altering the Western classical music environment is that students of color should just study the music of their respective "home cultures" if they want to be comfortable. In other words, why don't Black students just play jazz, for example? Aside from being segregationist, this argument ignores the fact that Western classical music institutions are explicitly recruiting these students because increasing demographic diversity has become an institutional core goal. This is an admirable goal that creates a moral obligation to maintain environments in which these invitees will thrive.

Even if one argues that the demanding nature of conservatory training makes it challenging for everyone to thrive, conservatory environments are currently designed to facilitate the thriving of some students more than others, depending on race, ethnicity, gender, sexual orientation, class, and disability. Additionally, the recruitment of a more diverse group of students is for naught if they cannot be retained to graduation, or subsequently leave the profession because of an accumulation of negative experiences.

Western classical music leaders should consider how identity threat and the constant perception of marginalization and assault undermines students' belief in themselves and contributes to academic and musical underperformance. The Eurocentrism of the curriculum, musical programming, and aesthetic environment directly contribute to this marginalization and the concomitant erosion of self-worth among these students.

Some of the most strident opposition to the messages expressed in this book might come from people of color, especially those who are professional musicians or have been professionally trained. But for many Black and Latinx musicians, as in other fields, the trade-off for high-level participation in a highly competitive and mostly white field has been to acculturate into a system that devalues nonwhite cultures. There is no getting around the fact that a system that devalues nonwhite cultures also devalues nonwhite identity. For some, the process of acculturation began very early if they were enrolled in a Western classical music program at a young age. For many of us, the process of acculturation occurs unconsciously.

Arguments justifying the preservation of the contemporary conservatory environment map onto strategies that protect the white racial frame: minimization, assumption of white moral virtue, and normalization. "The things you're talking about might happen, but they just aren't as bad as you claim." (Minimization.) "I think you might be misinterpreting. I know these white people, and they're not bad – they mean well." (Assumption of white moral virtue.) "Frankly, these challenges are in every field, and classical music is no different. This is just what people of color have to deal with to be successful." (Normalization.) The philosophy underpinning these responses leads to an unfortunate tendency among older musicians to cast young students of color as weak if they complain about Western classical music environments. Previous generations built character by struggling and surviving, and no less should be expected of a new generation, this thinking goes.

On Resilience

When I began working with conservatory students, I also believed that "dealing" with these environments was obligatory, just something we had to do in order to be successful. When Black students sought me out to express their frustrations, I pointed to examples of older Black people like my father, who grew up in the South, had a bachelor's degree from an HBCU, and a doctorate from an Ivy League daily, overt, and physically brutal racism to be successful. "Can you imagine how tough they are? That's how they succeeded!" I would say. This type of strength had always been necessary for Black people to succeed in environments that constantly belittled and diminished them, and I encouraged students to look to those examples. I was surprised and even a little offended at first when students pushed back against this argument. "But why should we have to do that?" one responded.

There is no doubt that individuals like these should serve as role models in many ways. But I eventually realized that my students were demonstrating strength, and not weakness, because they were demanding the right to be free from the obligation to tolerate racism in their environment. It wasn't that they lacked the character of previous generations; they were displaying strength of character by demanding the right to an environment that was designed for them to thrive, as any educational environment is supposed to be designed. As is the case for many Black people of my generation, my experiences and upbringing had conditioned me to approach racism and structural oppression as inevitable facets of modern American life, and that to triumph over these structures through professional success was the highest achievement. These students were demanding the right to be free of that struggle.

Obviously, being free of the need to struggle against racist oppression is a human right that we should take for granted. It is a sign of how far we are from being able to claim our full humanity that we are so challenged in imagining educational and artistic environments in which that struggle is no longer necessary.

On Freedom

The push for diversity is intertwined with another imperative: the search for spiritual and creative freedom. The restrictions on teachers and students evident in Western classical music pedagogy, in the working relationships between conductors, soloists and orchestra members, management and ensembles, boards and leadership, arise from the fact that the power relations of classical music are deeply conservative. Power is rarely shared; the autonomy of the collective is rarely respected; and the autonomy of the individual is dependent on social status. The right to power is conserved by classes that believe their positionality grants them a historical right to dictate the rules of engagement.

In such a fraught context, the individual performer rarely feels fully "free" as a creative entity. From student to grizzled professional, freelancer to tenured orchestral musician, at all points along this journey there are multiple power centers to appease, rules to learn and abide by fearfully, treacherous missteps to avoid. Control over employment opportunities and access to high-status individuals is shared sparingly and jealously guarded. These issues are partly a function of the economics of making art in a capitalist environment, to be sure, but also of the aesthetic style of engagement reflected in our performance and pedagogy.

In a class I teach, titled *Racial Politics of Classical Music*, we discuss the liberatory possibilities inherent in improvisation and the nature of the restrictive performance guidelines for through-composed Western classical music. I ask students to reflect upon these questions: How many times have you gotten on stage and truly *enjoyed* a solo performance? How many times have you felt totally free to express your personality, free of restrictions, free to simply present music that you love? How often are you totally focused on something other than the possibility of critique or failure?

The typical answer is: rarely. But how can we be surprised by this response when the performance experience is so deeply restricted, subject to intense critical examination on various social and political axes, and requires strict adherence to codes of conduct and

Conclusion 115

self-presentation that are increasingly at odds with students' cultural and personal values?

Once we begin discussing improvisation, I also ask students: How comfortable are you in just picking up your instrument and playing any notes that you choose? Can you select your own notes or do you require a formal plan to manipulate your instrument? Many students admit that they are deeply uncomfortable in stringing together self-selected sounds on their instrument. Consider the perversity of this situation: for years, students devote endless hours to practice, yet the end result is that many of them feel as if they literally cannot play a note, or at least, a note that has not been dictated to them on paper.

Freedom should be a principal object in the diversification of classical music. It is worth reflecting on to what extent the denial of social, political, cultural, and spiritual freedom characterizes the performance and pedagogy of Western classical music. Freedom equates with the empowerment of the individual musician to express their own core values, individuality, and personality through their music making, concomitant with the skills necessary to explore and deepen their understanding of their own values and personality through the making of music.

Index

Note: Figures are indicated by *italics*.

aesthetics 16–20; alienation 3–4; in African-American music 20, 22; in conservatories 9, 22; in culturally responsive pedagogy 37–42; in the curriculum 48; in fugitive pedagogy 3–37
Al Nour Wal Amal orchestra 73–4
antiblack 33, 35
Africana Studies 59
Africans 20, 41–2
Armstrong, E. 2
assimilation 3–4, 7–11, 13–19, 34, 102
ADHD 74–5

Bach, J. S. 28, 42, 56–7, 92, 96, 97
Baptist 87, 104
Baroque 14, 38–9, 56
Black 6–12, 15, 84–5, 95–109; Africans 41; blackness 11, 107, 108; composers 38–41, 96; music 20–2; singers 23; woman 85, 105; *see also* Black History Month; OCBMG
Bracey, J. 36
Beethoven, L. van 57, 92; sonatas 3, 29, 30–1; symphonies 99
BIPOC 1, 12, 63, 69
Black History Month 13, 34 *see also* Negro History Week
Blacking, J. 3
Black Lives Matter *35*

Bourdieu, P. 9
Brahms, J. 57, 96, 99
Brandenburg concerti, 30
Buechner, S. D. 70
Bull, A. 10, 30

Carlisle Indian Industrial School 14–16
cello 105
cisgender 69–71
concert dress 3, 48, 73
cultural appropriation 18; *see also* racial plagiarism
cultural deficit theory 37–8; *see also* cultural difference theory
cultural difference theory 37
culturally responsive pedagogy 9, 34–7; *see also* culturally responsive teaching
culturally responsive teaching 37

DEI 46–8, 52–5
diction 16, 19, 42
disability 64, 73–5
diversity 3, 5–7; capitulation 51; curricular 52, 96; in music theory 28, 41; as a question 6, 49; training 70
djembe 58
dominant 18, 33; in music 31
Dvořák, A. 96

Eastman 1
Eidsheim, N. 17
Ellington, D. 96
English 16, 33, 48, 87
ethnomusicology 57
equity 38, 62–6
Ewell, P. 28–9, 34, 41, 43; *see also* Feagin, J.; white racial frame

Feagin, J. 12, 27–8; *see also* white racial frame
Ferriday, Z. 8
Folk Song Symphony 39
fugitive pedagogy 9, 34–7

gender 22, 28–31, 48, 69–73, 103, 112
German 28–9, 31, 42–3
Givens, J. R. 35–6
Gottschild, B. D. 20–1
Guggenheim Fellowship 39

habitus 9
Hamilton, L. 2
Handel. G. F. 41
Harris, R. 39–40
Harvard University 33
Haydn, J. 29, 41, 57
Hanson, H. 39
heteronormative 62, 71–3
Hollywood 32
homophobia 62
Howard, T. 38
Hunter, D. 42

IBPOC 8
improvisation 58, 100, 114
Indiana 14
Indiana Manual Labor Institute 14

Jack, A. A. 2, 10, 78
James, R. 19
jazz 57, 84, 95, 97–9, 104, 111
Juilliard 1

Kang, J. M. 17–18
Kingsbury, H. 2–3

Ladson-Billings, G. 37
Latin music 92
Latinx 2, 6–9, 11–12, 37, 68, 78, 91, 105
LGBTQ+ 1, 62–3, 67, 69, 75
Lift Every Voice and Sing 36
Lind, V. R. 37
London 41

Marissen, M. 30
McClary, S. 30
McDonalds 10, 91
McKoy, C. 37
McKinley, W. 14
Marx, A. B. 30–1
Messiah 41
microaggressions 11–12, 47
midwestern 2, 104
misgender 69, 71, 72
misogyny 62
Monteverdi, C. 92
Mozart, W. A. 29, 41, 57, 92
musicology 27, 42–3, 56–7
music theory 28–34, 38, 41, 57; *see also* white racial frame

national anthem 36; *see also* Negro National Anthem
Native Americans 12, 14–16
Negro: History Week 34; National Anthem 36; voice 23
Nettl, B. 2, 8, 10, 24–5
neurodiversity 73–5
New England Conservatory 14, 46

Oberlin: Conservatory of Music 1–2, 14, 46, 58–60; African-American Music Minor 59; TIMARA Department of 20; *see also* OCBMG
OCBMG 69
Ohio 1
oratorio 92

orchestras 70–2, 74, 83–5, 94–104; fellowships in 7, 38

Palmer, R. 39
Piston, W. 39
Pham, M. H. 18
Price, F. 96
pronouns 70–2
Publius, X. 71
Puerto Rico 86–8, 91, 93
Pulitzer Prize 39

racial plagiarism 18
recitative 92–3
Reconstruction 14, 34
retention 1, 47, 51, 66
Rhapsody in Blue 39
Robinson, D. 8, 52
Royal African Company 41
Royal Academy of Music 41

Salaam, K. ya. 33
Scharff, C. 10, 30
Schoenberg, A. 30
Schumann, C. 39
Seeger, R. C. 39
Sessions, R. 39
sonata form 29–31, 92
South Africa 95
South Sea Company 41
Standard American English 33
Star Spangled Banner 36
Stormfront 8
Still, W. G. 39–40

Sweden 95
Symphony No. 1 "Afro-American" 39

Taylor, P. 17
Terry, C. 38
tonic key 30–3
transgender 62, 67, 69–71
transphobia 62
trombone 105
trumpet 95

violin 14

Walker, G. 39, 96
Western: aesthetics of 18, 21; canon 36, 41; classical music 6–8, 10–12, 30–1, 34; classical musicians of 56; education in 27, 46, 96, 113–14; tonality of 41
Winston, A. 14
white 8, 27–9, 34–6, 104, 106–8; *see also* white racial frame; white supremacy
white racial frame 27–9, 34, 42–3, 112
white supremacy 8, 19, 34, 48
Wilson, O. 20–1
Woodson, C. G. 13, 34–6

Yale 1

Zitkála-Šá 14, 17

For Product Safety Concerns and Information please contact our EU representative GPSR@taylorandfrancis.com
Taylor & Francis Verlag GmbH, Kaufingerstraße 24, 80331 München, Germany

www.ingramcontent.com/pod-product-compliance
Lightning Source LLC
Chambersburg PA
CBHW072219240426
43670CB00038B/2272